Mediterranean Villages

an architectural journey

Mediterranean
Villages

an architectural journey

steven & cathi house

Foreword by Lucy Ferrari

Introduction by James P. Warfield

First published in Australia in 2004
by The Images Publishing Group Pty Ltd
ABN 89 059 734 431
6 Bastow Place, Mulgrave, Victoria, 3170, Australia
Telephone (61 3) 9561 5544 Facsimile (61 3) 9561 4860
Email: books@images.com.au
Website: www.imagespublishinggroup.com

National Library of Australia
Cataloguing-in-Publication data

House, Steven, 1952– , House, Cathi, 1953– .
Mediterranean Villages: an architectural journey.

ISBN 1 86470 106 4.

1. Villages – Mediterranean Region. 2. Architecture –
Mediterranean Region. 3. Architects and community –
Mediterranean Region. 4. Mediterranean Region –
Description and travel. I. House, Cathi, 1953– . II.
Title.

720.91822

Edited by Eliza Hope
Designed by Steven and Cathi House
Final layout and production by The Graphic Image Studio Pty Ltd,
Mulgrave, Australia
Film by Mission Productions
Printed by Everbest Printing Co. Ltd. in Hong Kong/China

IMAGES has included on its website a page for special notices
in relation to this and our other publications. Please visit this site:
www.imagespublishinggroup.com

Contents

by Lucy Ferrari

Foreword

The creation of architecture demands a passionate concern for and knowledge of the environment. In order to achieve this knowledge and this concern, one must begin to see, and in doing so, to learn. According to H. Cartier-Bresson, "The drawing is a meditation, the photograph is an immediate action." *Mediterranean Villages: an architectural journey* is a perfect example of these two activities in combination.

It is my pleasure to write the foreword to this book on Mediterranean villages written, illustrated, and photographed by my former students Cathi and Steven House. I have known Cathi and Steven for more than 30 years. In 1968, my husband, Olivio Ferrari, and I began a study abroad program for students of architecture at Virginia Tech. Since then we have taken more than a thousand students to Europe with the goal of helping them learn to see, to see with more than their eyes, and to see beyond the surface of appearances.

Olivio once said "they look yet they do not see." Our task, our goal, was to help our students learn to see. Through travel and through a course I developed, Cultural Studies in Architecture, we helped them write about their daily experiences, the people they encountered, and the architecture of the cities and villages that they visited. Their journals, sketches, and photographs recorded the cultures and places they experienced and helped them on their journey into seeing.

When Olivio and I first came to the United States we felt prepared to share our knowledge and experiences with our students, but quickly realized how little we understood the culture of our host country. Our own experience of learning to see created one of the most interesting times of our lives and set the beginnings of what we would strive to teach our students. But how does one learn to see? From our base campus in Salzburg, Austria, we took the students to classical concerts in Baroque palaces, they rode their bicycles down a tree-lined allee to buy fresh pastries, sketched fountains in magnificent piazzas, wandered narrow alleyways to photograph details, studied German in lush gardens...For most of them this was their first cultural experience and for some it became the first step in a journey through life. One of our first European travel students was Steven House. His energy expressed itself in his sketches, photography, and writing. He was so eager to learn that he created a vocabulary for architecture in the German language and ultimately wrote his architecture thesis in German. This enthusiasm has continued throughout his life. After their marriage, Cathi and Steven spent a year abroad in Europe. This was the beginning of a lifetime of travel and study for them.

As one looks at this book one realizes that Cathi and Steven have certainly learned to see. Their drawings, words, and photographs show us ways of living through the people, the countryside, and the buildings they analyze. Each village they record presents a vision of the local culture and insights into specific architectural elements. One must love architecture to draw it in the way the Houses draw – meticulously. One must also have a passion for the details to take the photographs in this book. This is not just a book of drawings and photographs, but rather a compilation of life experiences, of a life of seeing. The Houses learned their lessons well. Their professional and personal lives are closely interwoven in their travels and their work, and they weave a beautiful story for us with their book. It presents villages with a sensitivity seldom seen, capturing the essence of architecture, and sharing a vision which has become their way of life.

Steven and Cathi have shared with us how much Olivio and I helped open their eyes and that we always travel with them in their hearts as they continue to explore the world and find new depths in their souls. Good teachers are like the sun...their students become their planets, revolving around their teachers until they are ready to become suns themselves. Cathi and Steven have become the sun and the young architects they mentor and the students whose lives they touch revolve around them now, learning, seeing, and opening their eyes to the possibilities.

by James P. Warfield

Introduction

For many, travel affords the opportunity not only to see new things and to explore different places, but also the time to clear the mind and to develop new visions. If one has the abilities to record and to process this new information through writing or drawing or photography, then travel can also provide a unique knowledge base upon which to build new theories. This seemingly unconventional process of self-education is unusually common among artists and architects, individuals in professions where travel becomes the medium for gathering visual and experiential precedents for developing thoughts and ideas that can be later interpreted and crafted into their own creative works. This role of "critical travel" is clearly demonstrated in the original graphic and built works of Steven and Cathi House. It is passionately recorded in *Mediterranean Villages: an architectural journey.*

I learned of Steven and Cathi's work in 1985 when I saw their insightful drawings and photographs for the first time. I felt an instant bond. I knew them both intimately through the products of their skilled hands and creative minds. Though separated by time and geography and age, we clearly shared the same professional passion for drawing, photography, and architecture, and we acknowledged travel as the matrix uniting these interests in a meaningful philosophy for living. We had experienced the same "dancing lessons."

A few months later, I invited them to show their traveling exhibit *Mediterranean Indigenous Architecture: timeless solutions for the human habitat* in the Temple Buell Architecture Gallery at the University of Illinois. I was teaching a graduate architecture theory seminar entitled "Form Determinants in Vernacular Architecture" and I recognized their recorded images of the Mediterranean as both profound and provocative. Their work had an historic sense of fit in the long tradition of past traveler/artists who have recorded special travel moments for future generations. I was intrigued with their abilities to capture the quintessential qualities of Mediterranean built form, the plasticity of stone and stucco surfaces washed in sunlight, so completely rendered in simple line drawings.

Of all the recurring topics of the fascination explored by architects for reference or inspiration, none is more enigmatic than the villages of the Mediterranean. In an architectural epoch which began with the tenet that architecture is a "machine for living" and has advanced to an age of computer technology, digital imaging, space-age materials, and critical path planning, what continues to draw architects to study these tightly clustered, irregularly planned, spontaneously developed anachronisms? Is it romanticism? Perhaps for some, but not many. Architects are by nature realists, rational thinkers, and problem solvers. Yet, not unlike the primitivists Picasso, Gauguin, Matisse, and others, who drew inspiration from the indigenous art of Africa and

Oceania, so numerous stalwarts in the development of contemporary architectural thought unabashedly cite the Mediterranean vernacular as critical in the shaping of their personal philosophies of architecture. Le Corbusier's travels as a young man in Southern Europe led him to studies of elemental geometric form and to a philosophy that would impact a generation. In simple geometric forms rendered in white and defined by intense natural light, he found "ordered chaos in the agglomeration of parts." Similarly, after traveling among the Greek islands, Edward Larabee Barnes expressed the principle of architectural continuity by use of fewer materials and the elimination of expressed articulation, "emphasis upon what is alike rather than different."

Nor has the Mediterranean vernacular been ignored as a theme of architectural exhibits and literature. In 1964, architectural critic Bernard Rudofsky in his exhibit *Architecture without Architects* shook the foundations of accepted architectural thought by utilizing Mediterranean villages, among other examples, to challenge directions in architectural education in general and in the teaching of architectural history specifically. Architect Myron Goldfinger published *Villages in the Sun*, a standard that dutifully distills the principles of design utilized in Mediterranean community architecture into understandable, usable terms for modern design. Norman Carver produced *Italian Hilltowns*, a photographic study that has become a classic, recording in sharp, hauntingly unforgettable images an

architectural planning genre that reflects an entire culture. And most recently, Paul Oliver assembled the most complete reference collection of vernacular architecture ever in his monumental effort *Encyclopedia of Vernacular Architecture of the World*.

So why, one might ask, would yet another book of village architecture be warranted, let alone compelling? *Mediterranean Villages* is both. Prepared from material developed from travel in four Mediterranean countries – Greece, Spain, Italy, and Yugoslavia – and based upon their traveling exhibit *Mediterranean Indigenous Architecture*, this remarkable volume offers a clear, fresh, compelling view of a timeless, even classic topic.

Much of the book's appeal derives from the appropriate variety of drawing and photographic techniques that Steven and Cathi employ. The collection is tightly formatted and presented in a cohesive, holistic manner. The drawings are exploratory, each prepared from a carefully selected viewpoint and for a specific purpose. They are successful not only as works of art, but also for the information and interpretation they provide. Cathi's one-point aerial perspective of Assisi, for example, communicates the magic appeal of many Mediterranean villages by appropriately emphasizing the openness of the piazza. The piazza is accurately portrayed in her drawing as the major negative space of the city – a tightly defined, uniquely described plaza resulting from the implosion of the negative space which flows from the

narrow winding constrained streets and alleys leading into it. By selecting a viewpoint which conceals all but a few of the other negative spaces within the town, she has produced an interpretive drawing which emphasizes the significance of the town's major public space by articulating not the plaza space itself, but the dense building forms tightly girded by Assisi's defensive wall. This same spatial concept is communicated at neighborhood and street scales in the facade studies of Mykonos. These lyrical line drawings detail architectural spaces for daily life. Human scale is revealed in the simple, rich details of everyday architectural features: a molded staircase, an arched entry, a shuttered door, a wooden balcony, a potted plant, a stucco bench.

The free style of the Assisi and Mykonos drawings sharply contrasts that employed by Cathi and Steven in their collaborative graphic interpretation of Dubrovnik. The presentation of this city is accomplished through a series of finely drafted architectural drawings, plans, and sections, which allows the viewer to understand the scale and fabric of the city and to discover the network of streets and public spaces that are its lifeline. The Dubrovnik drawings celebrate the architecture of the Mediterranean region, an aspect of culture frozen in time, and it is this clear focus that allows the variety of examples, scales, and presentation techniques to work. If the drawings of Dubrovnik demonstrate the Houses' abilities to produce exact and accurate graphic records for objective interpretation, the panorama of Santorini

offers yet another dimension of their work. Drawn by Cathi as much with the heart as with the hand, this is a wispy, even romantic, personal view of one of the Mediterranean's most visually charming architectural monuments. Saccharin street scenes of the Greek islands have long been the predominant subject of awed student travelers and tourist artists alike. Steven and Cathis' drawings transcend the superficiality of that drawing type by depicting in their Mediterranean examples those qualities of humanness in architecture that have been the hallmark of a search by many architects since the upheavals of the late 1960s. As with her drawing of Assisi, Cathi selected a unique viewpoint in order to present the agglomeration of buildings on Santorini as a comprehensible whole — and to communicate a concept undoubtedly shared and understood by countless other architects of generations past. Her interpretation of Santorini is at once a caricature of the Greek vernacular and a testimonial to the spirit of the builders responsible for one of the western world's remarkable indigenous building complexes.

Among the most intellectually satisfying drawings of the collection are Steven's procession series of the island villages of Paros and Mykonos. Skillful artists have long recorded the physical attributes of Mediterranean architecture: materiality, form, texture, and detail. It is through an architect's eye, however, that Steven addresses more abstract, experiential issues. His sequential sketches drawn as progressions through neighborhood lanes explore how we move through village space and how that movement, serendipitous or choreographed, contributes to an architectural experience. Steven captures the joy of wandering Greek village streets, the flow of rising up and descending gentle stairs, of anticipating what lies beyond the arched gateway, of discovering what might unfold around the next curved wall. His drawings reveal an architect's sensitivity to everyday movement and are a primer for understanding phenomenal space.

For those among us who feel that the sketch is the most highly interpretative, or perhaps only acceptable medium by which to study architecture, the photographs of Steven and Cathi House may provide pause. Their architectural photographs at every scale from the town views of Piran and Quesada to stairway details on Mykonos are evidence that the shutter may be mightier than the pen. In their hands, the lens, as the pen, is an exploratory instrument utilized to seek out and record new viewpoints. In one carefully selected set of photographs, they contrast the public stairways of three locations with clarity through creative editing. The stairways of Gubbio and Assisi in Italy and Mykonos in Greece are presented as architectural sculpture to be viewed and experienced. Each carefully selected photograph is a profound study of detail and creative expression in solving a most fundamental architectural problem.

In the final analysis, it is perhaps because indigenous Mediterranean architecture exemplifies those qualities that we value in any architecture that architects choose to study it. The Mediterranean towns are compact and concisely stated; their concept is clear. They utilize a consistent architectural vocabulary that accounts for great unity within complexity. Their structure and construction are honest, based upon straightforward decisions and local materials. They exhibit a richness of detail and expression, products of craftsmen who understood both the rules of their crafts and the principles of their culture and traditions. Finally, they reflect the humanness so greatly sought yet seldom achieved in architecture today. That Steven and Cathi House have been able to capture the essence of Mediterranean architecture is a significant achievement. Their drawings and photographs trigger memories for those who have traveled the Mediterranean and offer insight for those who have not. *Mediterranean Villages* is a handsome, meaningful record and a thoughtful interpretation of a classic theme. It is a gift shared by two talented individuals who understand the value of travel and how it has shaped their appreciation for a truly important architecture.

Italy

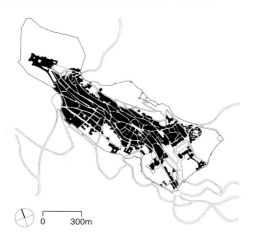

0   300m

Assisi

The delicate pink and white stones of Assisi bear the patina of age. Walls that sparkle brightly in the sun grow somber in the shadows. Assisi lies in long horizontal layers, rising through plazas and gardens to a breathtaking surprise when the view suddenly opens to soaring vistas over the surrounding countryside. The tranquil beauty of present-day Assisi lays gently over its embattled past and the medieval character that touches every corner, each narrow, twisting street. Unlike many towns in this region, Assisi does not cluster around a central, main plaza, but has many plazas, each shaped by the particulars of the roads that run into and through it and by the buildings necessitating its existence.

The ancient bell tower in the Piazza del Comune called to us, enticing us with the promise of a new perspective from above. It took weeks to arrange permission to enter the tower, formalities to respect, papers to sign. A fire had burned away the center of each level many years before, leaving only charred perimeters against which to lean very long wooden ladders. A crust, decades of pigeon droppings on each rung, spoke of infrequent use. The ladders were so long that at mid-span the beating of our hearts was enough to set them pulsating with movement, magnifying a general discomfort of heights into a spine-tingling fear. Had the climb itself not intensified our senses to maximum capacity, the view once we arrived would have. Sitting among the bells, which rang with intense force every fifteen minutes, we watched below the life of this splendid city, graced with beautiful churches and living streets and plazas, ebb and flow in the dance of daily life. We drew and dreamed and let that life flow through us, heightening our awareness and strengthening the foundations for our work as architects.

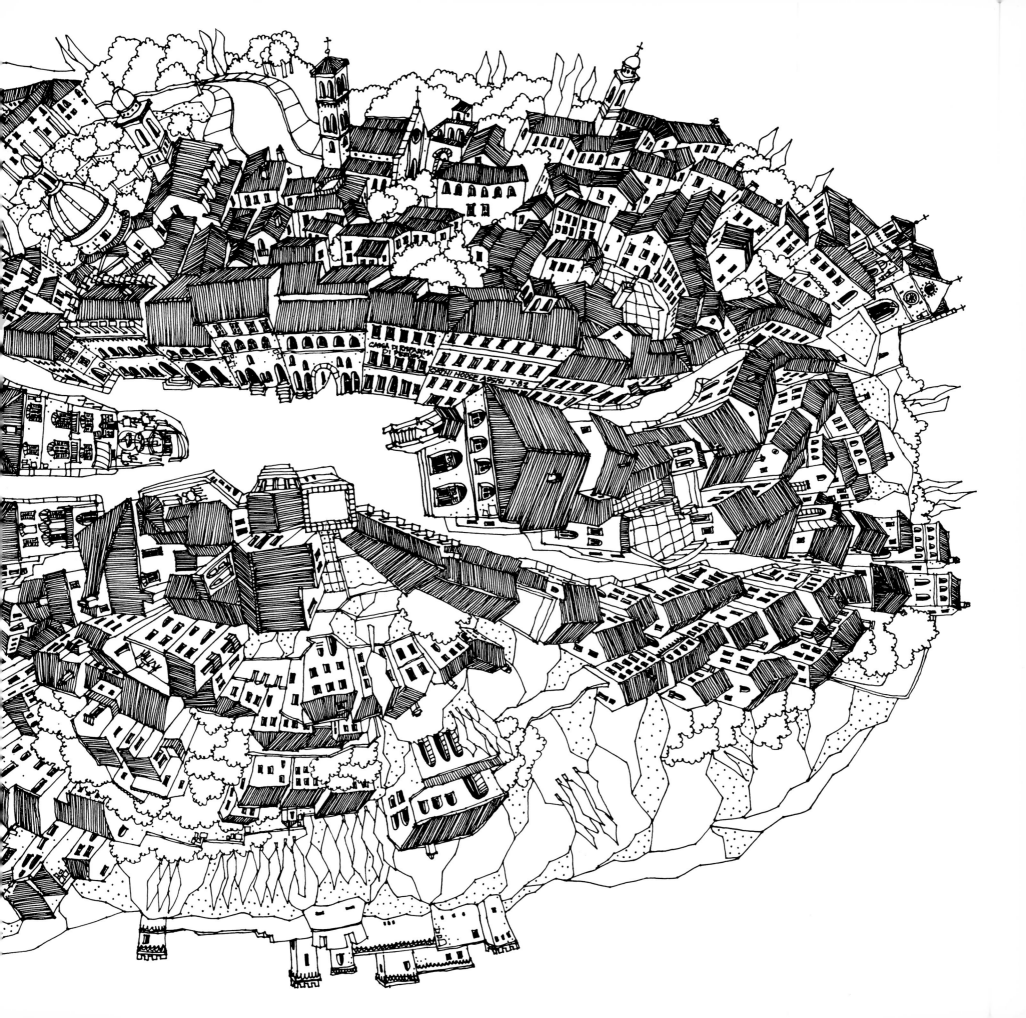

Movement is the guiding force behind not only the forms of the plazas, but the whole of this beautiful town. Stairways abound, each unique, each a piece of art in its own right — curving, soaring, ordering, sculpted, textured — adding surprise at every turn to the simple process of changing levels. Movement has shaped the buildings themselves as they are pierced with a passage or vault over a street. The powerful arch is everywhere, inviting movement, up, down, through. This piercing of the buildings allows for a three-dimensional complexity of form rarely encountered — streets and passages change direction without regard for the orientation or location of the buildings.

Around the plaza, clusters of chairs define a small world within, yet apart from all the hustle and bustle going on around it. The rich aromas of coffee, tiramisu, pizza, fresh bread, pastas invite a pause in the busy day's activities. Colorful awnings offer shady passage to cool interiors and the discovery of treats within. In the Piazza del Comune, the ancient fountain with its cool trickling water imbues the air with a serenity found in nature alongside a bubbling stream – a powerful reflection of nature in the midst of daily life.

1

2

3

4

5

6

"Serenity is the great

and true antidote

against anguish and

fear, and today, more

than ever, it is the

architect's duty to

make of it a permanent

guest in the home, no

matter how sumptuous

or how humble."

Luis Barragan

"The time of a work

holds its own validity

from which

the sense of truth

can be drawn

to inspire the work

of another time."

Louis Kahn

"But if it is only a small town or fortification, it will be better, and as safe, not for the streets to run straight to the gates, but to have them wind about like the course of a river. Besides appearing so much longer, they will add to the idea of greatness of the town. They will likewise conduce very much to beauty and convenience. Moreover, this winding of the streets will make the passenger at every step discover a new structure, and the front and door of every house will directly face the center of the street. But further, in our winding streets there will be no house but what, in some part of the day, will enjoy some sun, nor will they be without gentle breezes, and yet they will not be molested by stormy blasts, because such will be broken by the turning of the streets. Add to all these advantages that, if the enemy gets into the town, he will be in danger on every side from assaults from the houses." Alberti

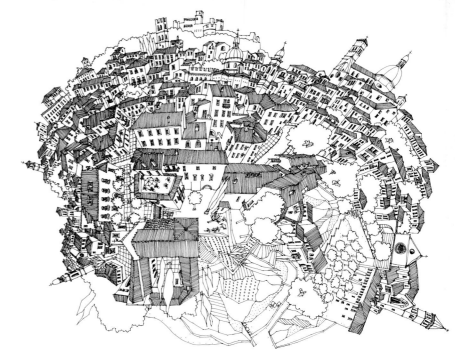

"The artist who works through the tradition projects his inner spirit upon the outside world. The receptive mind of the viewer, stimulated by his sense perceptions, internalizes the forms and completes the circle of communication. Beauty is objective, its focus lies within the object and not within the viewer, who may or may not be receptive and capable of understanding it. The master artisan participates in the creative process through traditional rituals which prepare him to create works of art that reflect in the world of the imagination. These rituals relate man to the rhythms of nature and the cosmos, whose solitude and serenity provide the first step in his spiritual ascent."

Nadar Ardalan & Laleh Bakhtiar

"Order and

proportion

are viewed

as cosmic laws

whose processes

man undertakes

to comprehend

through arithmetic,

geometry

and harmony.

Proportion

is to space

what rhythm

is to time

and harmony

to sound."

Nader Ardalan

Miranda

From a distance Miranda seems to hover somewhat above the mountain on which it is perched. Situated in an amphitheater-shaped outcropping projecting above the dense forest with a steep mountain on one side and sheer cliffs on the other, Miranda looks in on itself. This amphitheater form bounces and magnifies sound, yet the village has an air of peaceful serenity. Flocks of sheep pass through the main streets and the tinkling of their bells and soft cries are like music reaching into every corner. Sounds of construction, rhythmic chipping, and hammering feel like an embrace as the sounds come from every direction. The stone walls are plastered and colored in soft pinks, blues, and grays, faded and comfortable, at home in the present, yet carrying the past in their weathered skin for us to see and feel now. Perched above, watching the life of Miranda weave through the streets and plazas, listening to the calls of neighbors in greeting, of vendors announcing their arrival with freshly harvested produce or of services in sharpening or repairing, one can see the idea of "community" not only as a group of people who live near each other, but also as people who truly "live" together – with independent lives woven together into a unique pattern. Generations are laced together as well, with a last few proudly wearing the costumes of their time, as the youngest generation wears the latest in Italian high-style fashion. When we passed this way there were only four women left wearing the traditional clothing, each of them revered by their community as a precious treasure.

40

"The mystery of houses is the mystery of our mind. We move from room to room and only inhabit the present. Abandoned rooms are like abandoned thoughts, we can remember them and so we can return to them. As the shell of a house encompasses external rooms for our body, the shell of our body encompasses the interior rooms of our thought. We rummage through the attics of our souls as we rummage through the attics of our houses. The idea of a house is the idea of forever." John Hedjuk

"All faces are as old as the world." Picasso

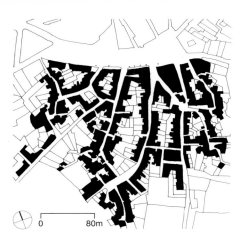

0   80m

Alberobello

At the heel of Italy in the region of Apulia, a forest of black conical roofs sprouts over the dazzling white town of Alberobello. As did many architectural traditions around the world, this building form developed as a tax-evasion tactic – the local official sidestepping taxes to the King on structures in his province by forcing the people to build without mortar so as to disassemble their homes into piles of stone and scatter into the woods when word of royal inspections came. Each thick-walled, round room has its own trullo roof of unmortared limestone. Larger rooms have larger cupolas – each house a collection of shapes and sizes of cones – the town an unbelievable chaos of variations. Each trullo is capped, some with a simple flat stone, some with elaborate pinnacles. Many trulli carry mysterious painted symbols surviving from ancient times. The trullo form was originally an agricultural structure and the countryside is still dotted with hundreds of beautiful trulli farmhouses. The swirling rings of stone are mesmerizing, the shape and size of each room a powerful contributor to the overall form of the town. The softly rounded walls of the buildings undulate in gently curving streets. All of the houses are the same yet each is unique.

"…in these we look for clues in our search for the proper balance between the individual parts and the harmonious whole."
Paul Mitarachi

"Establish beautiful masses, present pleasing contrasts, abolish multiple moldings. Lighting effects will offer sufficient variety. The hours of the day and night alone present so many possibilities. What diversity, when the rising sun spreads its shadow over the earth! What flickering effects when the moon traces labyrinths of light on the building." Ledoux

Even in more
conventional
construction, homage
is paid to the traditions
of history as a cone
sprouts through a flat
roof. This harmony of
repeated forms gives
rhythm to the ages, old
becomes new, new
becomes old, time can
be seen in the aging
color of the limestone
as cream slowly
changes to black.

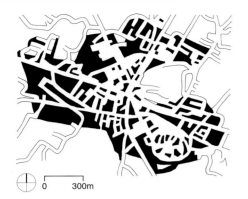

0   300m

Locorotondo

Not far from Alberobello, crowning a gentle hill, is the circular town of Locorotondo, The five o's in its name reflect its crazy, round shape. The exterior walls of the tightly clustered perimeter homes form the defensive structure, with arched openings leading to the center of town. Built from the same materials as Alberobello, the results are quite different. Buildings are tall, braced with arched passages and graceful buttresses. The black limestone roofs are steeply pitched with occasional references to the trullo form. Lined with brilliant white houses and flower-filled balconies, the winding flagstone streets open suddenly at the edge of town to offer spectacular views over the countryside.

Random surprise is the result of an organic transformation of material to form; form that is the result of complex needs – the need for shelter, private and public spaces, place to worship, place to sleep. All the needs of human existence direct the formation of stone into walls – and with that the development of the space between walls into rooms sheltered within – or the development of the spaces between as passage...with openings in the walls for light, air, views. Architectural form developed first from need – then needs demanded more and artistry began – and from that artistry a demand for poetry in the human interaction with walls. To walk the streets of villages like Locorotondo is to walk the dance of life. In the streets of Locorotondo a curve invites wonder, a shaft of sunlight or an ornate molding draws the eye, the street opens suddenly into a market or a plaza...wandering the streets can be an adventure if we let it be so, if we allow wonder, amazement, surprise to guide our steps.

Rhythms
of buttresses
invite passage.
They provide
a ceiling
enclosure
that feels
like an embrace.
Every few steps
the view changes
as each buttress
or arched opening
frames a completely
new view.
An arch can hold
enormous weight.
It can frame our world.
Its soft form is calm,
embracing
protective
safe.
Buttresses,
fragments of arches,
march along a passage
giving rhythm,
order,
enclosure,
so that the
uncontrollable chaos
of life can happen
embraced.

"Within the cityscapes surfaces are developed like the skin of the body which both hide and reveal the anatomical structure, like the skin of the pomegranate. The richness of both appear only on the inside, where lie the delicate seeds of life and its true color."

Nadar Ardalan & Laleh Bakhtiar

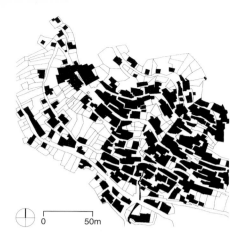

0   50m

Pesche

The gray stone of this almost deserted village blends into the mountainside to which it clings. Pesche first presents an almost chameleon-like texture, for, from a distance, though the village is in clear view, it is almost impossible to discern. What seems to be an unnatural ordering of stone patterns on the cliff face transforms into a dense, vertical, austere world. In the stillness of sound and the harshness of the gray stones, senses feel muted and life seems to go on at a rhythm detached from the rest of the world. Time does not exist here – only the eroding forces of the weather returning these stones to the cliff from which they were carved.

Sitting quietly and watching the air shimmer, thick and transparent, reflecting a softening veil over everything, making the world feel more a photograph than real, there is a clarity revealed by this veil. This softening blurs away distractions such as dirt or weeds or irregular finishes. The calls of mules, roosters, and pigeons, the sounds of old women sweeping the streets and pouring water over their thresholds, children laughing...all sounds are amplified and at the same time muted by this shroud of full, rich air.

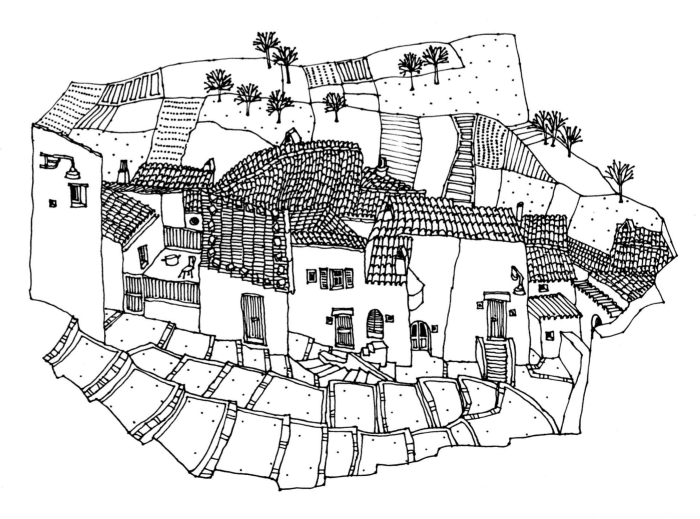

Within the village

ancient ruins

and inhabited houses

are meshed together

into a quiet calm.

Local women gather

to do their laundry

at the public fountain

beside the remains

of the castle

— now inhabited by

mules and chickens.

Rugged textures

of every surface glint

as the sun

rakes across,

adding sparkle

to materials

that do not seem

as though they could

sparkle,

bringing

into question

even the most basic

understanding

of material

solidity

and transparency.

"The tower stood among the houses in the street like Sunday among the days of the week. And I, my eyes darting down the rows of houses, started scanning this living calendar for the first major holiday. And I found it." Milorad Pavic

"The sum total of man's created efforts is nowhere more explicitly manifested than in his settlements. Villages, towns and cities, through the arrangement of distinct building types assembled from temporal forms, magnify these human artifacts through repetition, creating images on a super human scale. Here too, the world of similitudes guides the ultimate formation, the city taking form almost as though a shadow were taking focus with the shape that cast it."
Nadar Ardalan & Laleh Bakhtiar

Carpinone

Deep in the center of Italy, in the heart of Molise, near Isernia, small fairytale villages crown almost every hill. From each village the vista over the surrounding countryside includes numerous other villages, each complete with towers, castles, church bells, and markets. Centuries of struggle among these rival communities has long passed and the residents now live peacefully in their charming worlds. Spreading across two intersecting hills topped with church and castle, Carpinone is woven together with steep-staired walkways. On ancient doorsteps the custom of lacemaking survives as grandmothers pass the tradition on to young girls. The clicking of bobbins resounds in the narrow alleyways, a unique communal music binding the generations together.

One day the circus came to town and everyone was abuzz with excitement. The circus comes infrequently so it is a rare treat. Enticements came all day – animals paraded through town, a worn truck drove back and forth loudly announcing the performances in glorious descriptions. Children followed, dancing with glee; parents gathered on doorsteps to watch, marveling and imagining how magical it would be. This was the Circus Winter, a family who share all of the various tasks – the clown sold tickets and was master of ceremonies, the lion tamer ushered everyone to their seats, the acrobat handed out popcorn and drinks. There were three rows of seats with prices varying slightly depending on the row chosen. We joined a sellout crowd of 30 spectators to wait in breathless anticipation. The clown, who couldn't hold onto anything, generated peals of laughter. A pony trotted around the ring, jumping over tiny obstacles to waves of clapping. The acrobat, in her pink tights and tutu did backbends, the splits, and several interesting moves with a large ball, all to enchanted onlookers. During an hour-long intermission all family members laboriously erected a rickety cage inside the ring. A tired and mangy lion was prodded into running around the perimeter and jumping onto boxes to rest for a moment, all of this taking less than fifteen minutes, after which the cage was laboriously taken down while the acrobat performed a few more backbends, to the delight of the crowd. It was a successful evening for everyone. The parents and children meandered home, their thoughts soaring with the magic they had just witnessed. The tent disappeared before midday to move onto the next village.

Sitting down on the stepped walkway to sketch,

an apron full of peas are deposited into my lap

before I can extract my sketchbook.

I look up into the smiling face

of my new afternoon companion.

She sits on her stoop

and we shell peas together, and,

with no common language between us,

we discuss life and love, home and family,

and the beauty of the world around us.

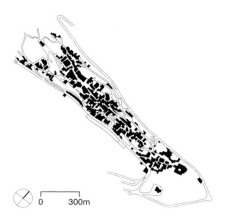

0   300m

Calascio

The dark stones of Calascio cling to the mountain below the Rocca – a menacing, jagged silhouette of the ancient castle and the town around it. With the Gran Sasso mountains as its backdrop, the setting is spectacular. Calascio's circulation pattern consists of horizontal roads following the contours of the hill, with a veritable maze of interconnecting stairs and vaulted passages. The tinkling bells of sheep as the flocks pass through town on their way to graze, the aroma of fresh breads and homemade pastas, the calls of the produce man as he makes his daily rounds – all are integral parts of this peaceful village.

We arrived just before dark in this tiny, remote village with no idea of what, if any, accommodations we might find. With few lights on we headed to a little bar where everyone contemplated where we could sleep. Calls were made and soon an old man arrived who walked slowly in front of our car to show us the way. Two rotund sisters, Pia and Maria, greeted us with enthusiasm and we found a comfortable home in their care. The ceiling of our room was painted with all the moldings and shadows that might have existed, but did not. Our balcony overlooked the entire town. Their kitchen was a veritable museum of kitchens through the ages – from wood burning below a massive ceramic bowl to the latest in contemporary Italian appliances – all working and each chosen carefully for the appropriateness of the meals they prepared for us each day. A peek into what we assumed might be a pantry was greeted with a rush of cool air, and there before us was the face of the cliff, right behind the door, with fresh cold water seeping into a pitcher. Pia and Maria's lives revolved around us during our stay, each day filled with the joys of finding just the right ingredients and preparing the perfect meal.

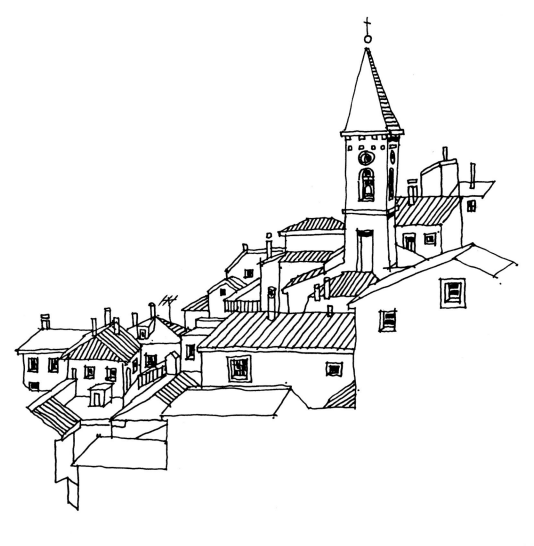

With few cars in Calascio Pia and Maria were overjoyed when we offered to drive them wherever they wanted. On a long, slow drive through high mountain meadows surrounded by the peaks of the Gran Sasso, we were sprinkled with a flurry of snow, glistening in the sun like so many jewels tossed on the emerald carpet of grass. At a visit to a nearby cheese factory our car was loaded almost beyond capacity, followed by a visit to their old friends – where we were treated to paper thin wafers embossed and prepared by hand in the fireplace as they talked. The family business, many generations old, was blacksmithing and as the happy sisters visited their friends we lost ourselves in the workshop, examining amazing fragments of work on the walls, the floor crunchy with cinders underfoot, feeling, as we touched these dusty pieces, the hands that had formed them.

"Concerned with form and with the shape of objects surrounding us - that is, with design - we will have to look at the things we have made. With the evidence of our work before us, we cannot escape its verdict. Today it tells us of separateness, of segregation and fragmentation." Anni Albers

"It is always difficult to comprehend one's own time. Because, living in it, the presuppositions of beliefs are obscured by their very familiarity; the customary is outside the realm of questioning and so is easily overlooked. What we are clearly aware of today is our feeling of amazed confusion. A decisive aspect of this general feeling of instability is due to today's technique of communication. Since it stresses the moment, it accelerates the process of rise and fall of ideas. We see different beliefs in quick succession or simultaneity, contradicting each other, overlapping each other. Faced with such devastating multiplicity, we are often forced to submit to indecision or to opinions, easily changeable, not worth being called convictions." Anni Albers

"Though only the few penetrate the screen that habits of thought and conduct form in their time, it is good for all of us to pause sometimes, to think, wonder and maybe worry; to ask 'where are we now?'" Anni Albers

0   80m

San Stefano

From a distance San Stefano looks like the classic fairytale village with gray stone houses clustered around a tall, cylindrical tower. In a dramatic setting against the Gran Sasso mountains, this hilltop village offers striking views to the countryside. Subdued and partially abandoned, remnants of more prosperous times are found in the empty piazzas and crumbling passageways. San Stefano belonged to the Barons of Piccolomini from Siena until it was purchased in 1569 by Francisco de Medici of Florence, under whose protection the wool trade flourished until the end of the 18th century when it passed on to the King of Naples. The cylindrical tower, built by the Medici, is unique in this region. For thousands of years shepherds have moved their flocks back and forth through this territory, from the mountain pastures to the wide plains of Apulia, influencing the economy, the culture, and the lifestyle of the inhabitants. The decline of the village began at the end of the 19th century when an exodus reduced the population to less than two hundred, mostly farmers who are well known throughout Italy for their lentils.

From the tower it is easy to
observe in the paths below
patterns of movement that
lace this community together,
paths that move with the terrain,
that split and merge, and wrap
around buildings and gardens,
that terrace and splay and give
moment for pause, a place to
visit with a neighbor, or to rest,
or just to admire the view
and the way the sun sparkles
on the rugged mountains.

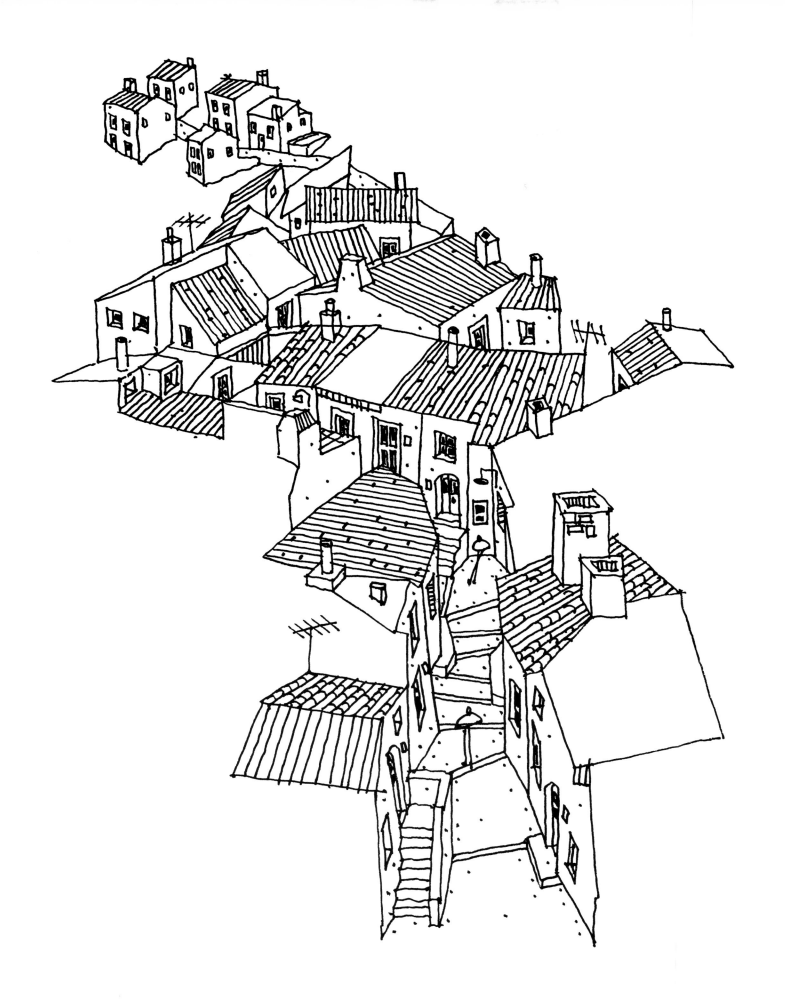

"I believe in the fairy tale.

I believe in the wish of the

fairy tale as the beginning of

science. Reality is the dream.

Reality is the fairy tale.

Art is the giver of light." Louis Kahn

San Gimignano

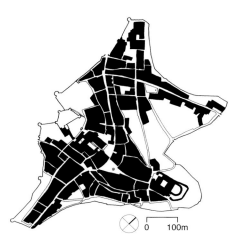

0 — 100m

In the golden Etruscan countryside, surrounded by fields of Chianti vineyards, the towers of San Gimignano are visible for miles. On a hilltop between Florence and Siena, this 14th-century town is one of the purest gems of the past. Ramparts still encircle the town, preserving its picturesque medieval appearance. Fourteen tall towers, originally seventy-five, were built in the Middle Ages by noble families for use as keeps during the constant struggles. Many of the towers are leaning – some say due to subsidence, others that they were designed that way to prove the skill of the architect. The narrow streets of San Gimignano are lined with golden limestone palazzos and the charming piazzas are alive with flowers and bustling activity. The stone walls seem to glow from within, casting a tangible light onto all who pass, enveloping them in a warm embrace. The curving of the streets offers a constantly changing view yet gives gentle reminders of orientation. Flowers cascade from window boxes and cluster at little stands. Sound bounces through the streets, transforming all sounds into a music of life.

"Architecture is form

placed between the

ground and the sky."

Eero Saarinen

"Order and proportion are viewed as cosmic

laws whose processes man undertakes to

comprehend through arithmetic, geometry and

harmony. Proportion is to space what rhythm is

to time and harmony to sound." Nadar Ardalan & Laleh Bakhtiar

MORTE DEI
PALAZZI
DI
SIENA

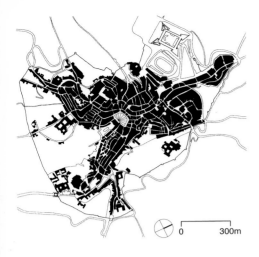

0 300m

Siena

98

In the midst of the Tuscan countryside, the narrow streets of Siena meander peacefully over three converging hills. Medieval palaces, walls, towers, and gates stand now, as they have through the ages, as a testament to the power of man's ability to create extraordinary richness through thoughtful constructions for life's simple necessities. Siena is a place of profound serenity, inviting contemplation and wonder. The town as a whole is consistent in its scale, colors, and use of materials, laying a perfect backdrop for the extraordinary architectural masterpieces sprinkled like gems throughout the town. Siena's magnificent Duomo is a visual fantasy with bold bands of black and white marble and facades and buttresses encrusted with intricate carved figures and stone lacework. At every step the palette in this magnificent construction becomes more and more fantastic, even down to the artistry of the floors. The shell-shaped Piazza del Campo is one of the great gathering places of the world, its harmonious curving facades culminating in the massive Palazzo Comunale with its Torre del Mangia soaring to 335 feet/102 meters. The paving of brick and stone is set in a radial pattern that pulls and twists the occupants in a subliminal dance.

Every summer the Piazza del Campo is transformed
on July 2 and August 16 for the celebration of the Palio,
a horse race that pits neighborhoods against each
other. The 17 Districts each send representatives who
display their colorful banners in a parade around town
before the thunderous race around the perimeter of the
piazza, a race looked forward to all year, greeted with
intense enthusiasm, which lasts only a few moments.
We had the pleasure of being in Siena for the race, a
mad event, when the piazza is filled with sand and soil
to cushion the hooves. The soil is watered to keep the
dust down, but the slippery mess becomes its own
hazard as people jostle for position awaiting the event.
After the race the sinuous streets are filled with blocks
of long tables and feasting continues till dawn.

"In the realm of the incredible stands the marvel of the emergence of the column. Out of the wall grew the column. The wall did well for man. In its thickness and its strength it protected him against destruction. But soon, the will to look out made man make a hole in the wall, and the wall was very pained, and said, 'What are you doing to me? I protected you, I made you feel secure – and now you put a hole through me!' And the man said, 'But I will look out! I see wonderful things, and I want to look out.' And the wall still felt very sad. Later, the man didn't just hack a hole in the wall, but made a discerning opening, one trimmed in fine stone, and he put a lintel over the opening and soon, the wall felt pretty well. The order of making the wall brought about an order of wall making which included the opening. Then came the column, which was an automatic kind of order, making that which was opening, and that which was not opening. A rhythm of openings was then decided by the wall itself, which was then no longer a wall, but a series of columns and openings. Such realizations came out of nothing in nature. They came out of a mysterious kind of sense that man has to express those wonders of the soul which demand expression." Louis Kahn

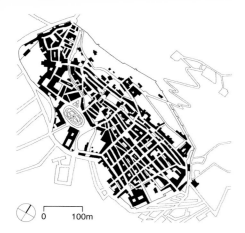

0   100m

Gubbio

In the austere grandeur of a dramatic, treeless site at the mouth of a gorge on Mount Ingino, Gubbio has been called the City of Silence, as it feels to be forgotten by the passage of time. The remains of a well-preserved Roman theater from the time of Augustus mark a period of growth and expansion for a city the Romans called Iguvium. As can many Umbrian towns, Gubbio traces its origins to the Etruscan era. Remnants of history abound in statues and moldings, cut stone and rubble walls, Gothic windows and Renaissance balconies, graceful arches and powerful buttresses, loggias and courtyards, Gothic cathedrals and holy monasteries. Overlooking a fertile plain the ramparts and towers, palazzos and piazzas give Gubbio a majestic feel with wide boulevards and graceful sweeping stairs, complemented by intimate cobbled lanes and dark arched passages. Many houses still have two doors – one for everyday use – the other, door of death, through which coffins were brought out. Rugged stone walls are softened with the gentle swaying of laundry and textured with brick patches, marking that which was, with that which is new.

"Landscape framed in an open doorway. The sunlight licks the floor in a thin gold line, and slowly creeps up the wall. The landscape comes so much closer to us like this, closer than when we try to see it through a wide opening, in an unending continuity, or behind a great sheet of glass, or standing in a house with glass walls, in which we would no longer know if we are within or without. Here the landscape comes near us, it comes into the building, not so much that we see it with our eyes, but more because we know it exists, we capture its existence with all our senses, we embrace it with our body and soul." Aris Konstantinidis

Greece

Meteora

Delphi

Athens

Corinth

Dimitsana

Stiminitsa

Anditsana

Sparta

Monemvasia

Mykonos

Paros

Sifnos

Amorgos

Ios

Santorini

Crete

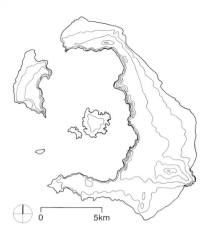

0 5km

Santorini

Rising from the deep blue water of the Aegean to almost 1,000 feet/300 meters, the sheer cliffs of an ancient volcanic crater, topped with sparkling white villages, are one of the most spectacular sights in the Mediterranean. Thirty-five hundred years ago Santorini, or Kaliste, as it was then known, was occupied by a flourishing culture that reveled in the arts. Murals have survived that depict dancing and fishing, beautiful gardens, and exotic animals. Hot and cold running water and a complex waste disposal system made for comfortable living. Trade with far ranging cultures is evident by those fragments of daily life left behind. That world was shattered in 1450 BC when a catastrophic eruption blew the center out of the island, and covered what remained with ash hundreds of feet deep. Left barren for centuries, the island was eventually reoccupied by Phoenicians, Spartans, who named the island Thera after their leader, Dorians, Egyptians, Romans, Naxians, Italians, Turks, and the Venetians, who named the island Santorini – after Saint Irene of Thessalonika, the island's patron saint who died there in 304.

Several fragments of the original island, pieces of the volcano's rim projecting above the flooded crater, or caldera, have survived. The largest of these is the island of Santorini or Thera, as it is also known, a smaller island, Therasia, just large enough to have its own village, a tiny islet, and the volcanic center where two barren lava masses shudder and spout from time to time, reminders that this is still an active volcano. Scientists have studied the volcano in depth and, from the evidence of the extraordinary power of that eruption, have related it to such events as the parting of the Red Sea, the sinking of Atlantis, and to the destruction of the Minoan civilization of Crete. Ash from the eruption has been found in Egypt and evidence of tidal waves from the explosion as far away as Spain. The 32-square-mile/83-square-kilometer caldera is more than 1,312 feet/400 meters deep, so deep that ships cannot anchor and must be tied to buoys.

Our first image of Santorini was on a poster in our hotel room in Athens. Days spent exploring classical architecture gave way to dreams of unimagined beauty and wonder stimulated by this photograph of a place that seemed too magical to be real. Visions of children playing with oranges, the cacophony of a dozen radios, each tuned to a different station, holding on to our seats as the boat pitched through rough seas, watching a crowd of men herd a very large pig into the lower deck of the ship, weave through our memories of the thirteen hours it took the boat to reach Santorini.

Arriving just before midnight, it looked as though, high in the heavens above us, the stars had gathered into a twinkling line — the lights of Thira, or Fira as it is also called, the island's main village clinging to the cliff a thousand feet above us. In the dead of winter there were few travelers and few facilities available. Wandering the streets, inquiring in shops, we eventually met someone who knew someone who had the keys to a hotel, closed for the winter. They handed us the keys and invited us to make ourselves comfortable. When morning arrived and we stepped out onto our balcony, we found ourselves face to face with the view from that poster — and seeing it there before us, it still seemed too fantastic to be real. Below the balcony was a staircase, seemingly carved from the face of the cliff, meandering this way and that. It was our first view of the Greek Island vernacular, and in that moment our lives were changed forever.

We settled into an 800-year-old house clinging to the cliff 1,000 feet/300 meters above the Aegean, part cave, part built, a terrace facing west, islands floating in the distance. In those months as we explored, drew, and photographed, we learned to see, to feel, to experience architecture. Our days were filled with discovery, amazement, and an overwhelming realization of the power architecture can have if thoughtfully conceived. With none of the amenities normally used to define civilized living, we learned what civilized living really was, or at least what it should be. Thick walls kept us warm on cold nights, cool on warm days. A large concrete bowl kept our food chilled. Whitewashed walls amplified daylight to fill our rooms. During those quiet days of climbing and sketching, our souls as architects were born. Those lessons guide us still, everyday.

With few trees
and no
natural
water supply,
the inhabitants
developed
a stone vault
roof system,
forming their homes
and the whole village
to catch and store
every drop of rainwater.
The result is
a beautiful confusion
of vaults and patios,
an endless array
of drains,
directing the rainwater
into cisterns.
In the process,
they have created
a sculpted world,
fluid in form,
unencumbered with
concepts like
uniformity,
symmetry,
property lines...

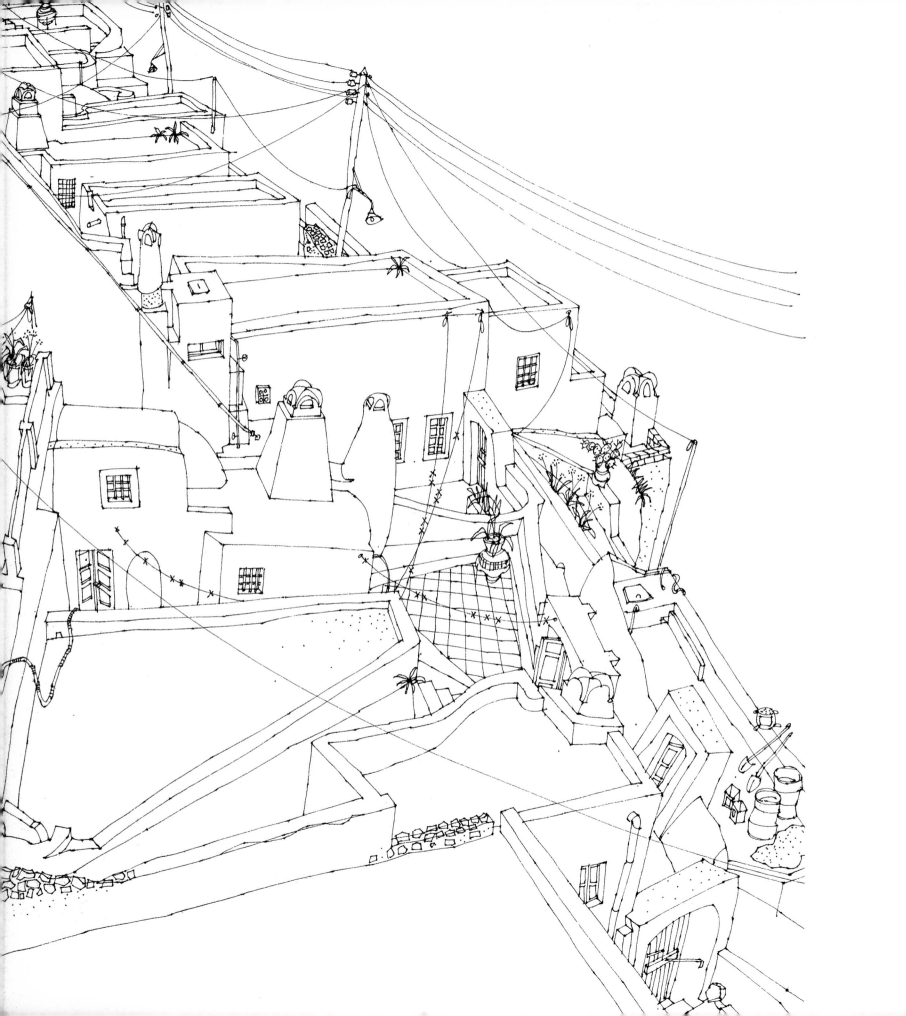

Fluid forms flow, seep, vault...
Stairs climb over roofs,
over abandoned caves.
A place to wash clothes
built into a terrace wall
offers the most spectacular
of views while tending
to the most mundane of tasks.
With every few steps
the path changes direction,
opens to constantly changing
views, exposing, hiding, opening,
closing...every path an adventure,
to be experienced over and over,
never the same, always new.

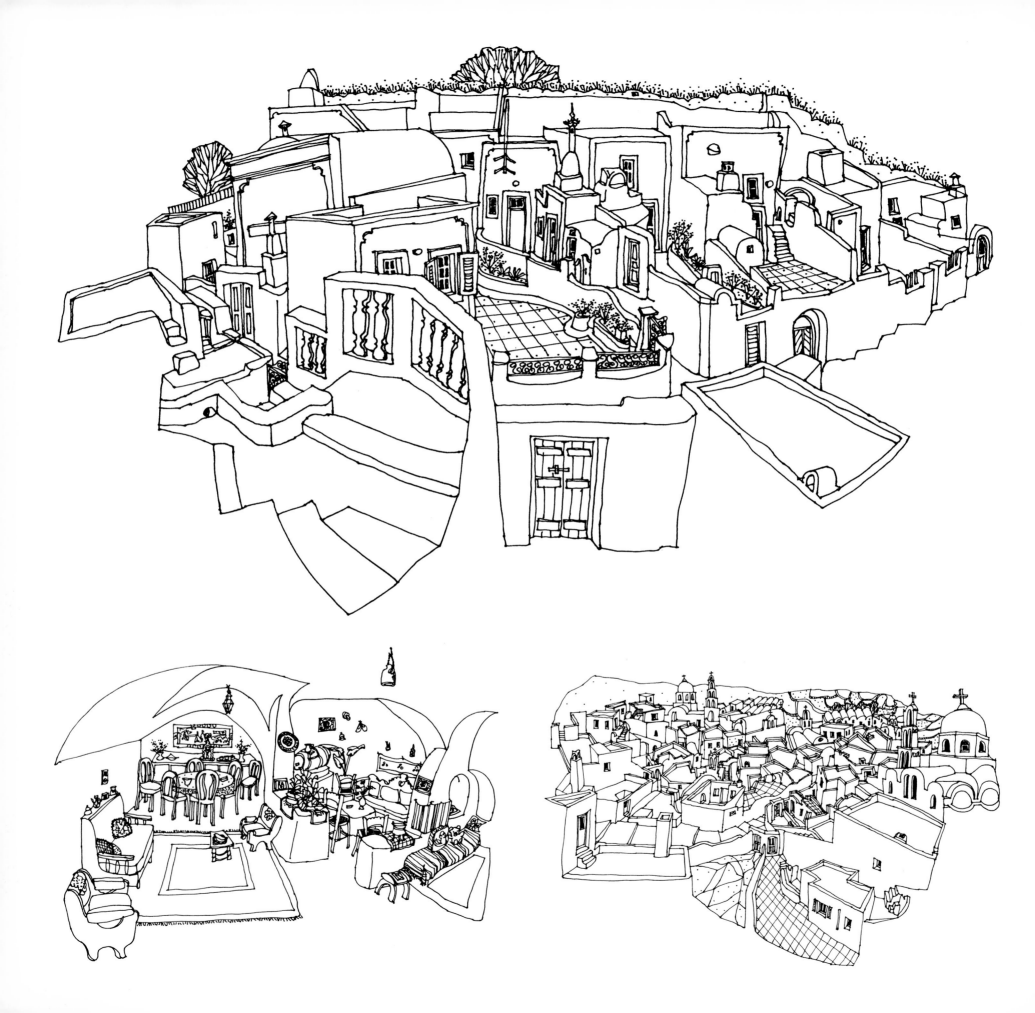

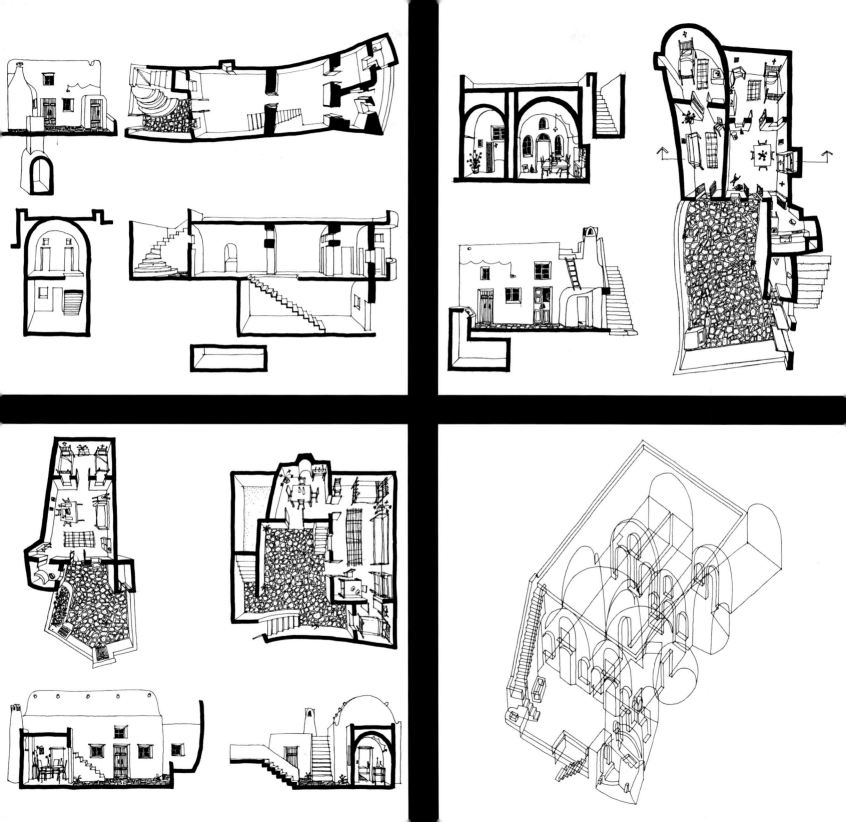

"Therefore

true architecture

is not that which

stands forever

steady and static in

its functional character,

its shape and form,

but which lives in time,

because it is born

and reborn —

not a being

but a becoming."

Aris Konstantinidis

"The Greek landscape

affects man's spirit —

his soul and his body

and his most secret thoughts —

like music.

The deeper you feel it

the more you grow attuned to it,

ever discovering in it

new elements of balance and freedom."

Katzantzakis

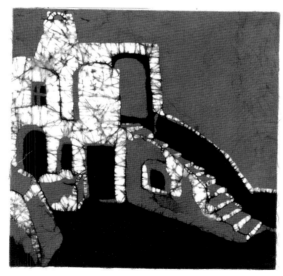

 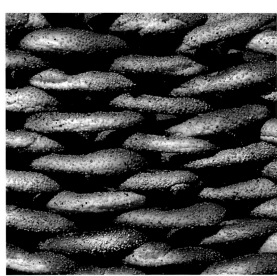

"The stone you hold in your hand has power over you; for it has a voice of its own."

Papadiamandis

"Landscape and man;

these are the two

primary factors

for the creation

of a true work of architecture.

There can be no architecture

without a landscape

to build in…

But land, landscape,

natural surroundings:

these words imply

a certain kind of

natural material,

the predominant material

that the land has to offer.

This is the material

that man uses to build

and shape his structures...

This goes for the simplest

stone sheep feld

or wall or building

of the most elaborate edifice."

Aris Konstanidis

"Today stands

between yesterday

and tomorrow,

today is the connecting link

between what is gone

and what is to come.

The preceding age

passes on its forms

to the present age,

which in turn

passes it on

to the following period,

just as the truly modern

is both past and future,

old and new."

Aris Konstantinidis

Silence.
We had never heard silence before.
No electricity humming through wires in the walls.
No water flowing through pipes in the walls.
No appliances, no motors, no machinery.
Meter-thick stone and earthen walls to muffle any sounds outside.
High, cross vaulted ceilings to scatter sounds inside.
The feeling of pressure against our eardrums,
like on a plane when landing,
making us feel something was wrong with our ears.
Then, suddenly, we could hear our heart beating,
and the waves a thousand feet below,
and the distant, soft moan of a ship's horn approaching,
and the breeze among the leaves,
the beetle crawling on the terrace,
the flower opening, the star twinkling...
as though a whole new sense was born.
We could suddenly hear life.

"Our future days stand before us – like a long row of lighted candles – warm, golden candles, full of life." Cavafy

"A rock

as it emerges

from the sea;

above

the most luminous

of skies;

this is the land —

Greece,

birthplace of beauty,

measure,

and balance,

of authenticity,

artistic vision,

and spiritual ethos.

But beyond that,

the clarity

of the atmosphere

of this land.

More than anywhere

else on earth,

each thing

is allowed to stand out

clearly,

revealing its modeling,

its contours,

both in its own

separate entity,

and in relation

to all other things."

Aris Konstantinidis

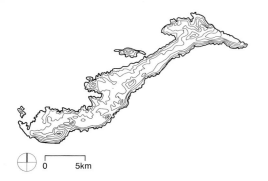

0   5km

Amorgos

Three stark, austere peaks of an oblong mountain range soaring as high as 3,000 feet/914 meters are the stony spine that is the island of Amorgos. Inhabited since prehistoric times, the remains of three important ancient cities speak of grandeur that cannot be felt in the flower-filled lanes of the picturesque villages. A peaceful serenity envelopes ancient Minoa with its ruins of a gymnasium, a stadium and a temple to Apollo, Arkessini with its fortifications and burial sites, and Egiali, an ancient harbor where the ruins of the fortress are all that remain. The main village of Khora is a maze of twisting walkways wrapping simple homes and forty churches and chapels around and through the 13th-century Venetian fortress. One chapel is so tiny only two can fit inside.

The winter chill keeps most travelers away so the island is quiet as we nestle into the cluttered room of the daughter, now married, of the elderly couple who welcomed us into their home. Evening conversations range around the globe, even though they had never left this tiny place. Crystaline air glints off the ripples in the sea as we breathe deeply the salty air and feast on chips, omelettes, and pan-seared fish, caught within reach of where we sit. A bumpy ride in the back of a truck across rough terrain was the main form of transport, at least where trucks could pass. Perilous climbs in a cloud of fragrance from wild herbs crushed under foot are necessary to reach some of the architectural jewels. Once covered with dense oak forests, a 19th-century fire stripped the island and revealed the rugged terrain of today. In a magnificent setting, the monastery of Panagias Khozoviotissas, a massive fortress built in 1088, clings to a barren cliff rising from the sea. The monks within graciously welcome any who make the journey to their door, offering refreshment and lively stories. Precious, even miraculous, icons, ancient manuscripts, and much revered religious artifacts are protected within the massive walls.

Two women, long-time friends, sharing a gentle world where morning walks include collecting wild herbs, thyme and oregano releasing their pungent bouquet, traded later in the day for fresh fish or homemade cheese...Two amazing women with fascinating stories to tell, living quietly in the ruins of what once was the castle, surrounded by their memories and a collection of drawings and paintings gathered from random encounters with artists who venture into their world. Their stories speak of adventures normally only found in fairytales. Their collection speaks of many who have passed through this remote area. A cup of tea offered and taken gives pause to our own adventure as we slipped for a while into theirs, their adventures now a part of our own, with shared memories of magic and tea and a drawing left with them to mark our passage there.

In these villages,
buildings and passages
each follow their own patterns,
sometimes seeming
to be unaware of each other.
In our world
towns are planned,
streets are laid out,
zones are assigned;
in these villages
the overlap is more organic.
Buildings twist and turn,
step and vault,
turning at the whim of the terrain,
of the winds, of the sun,
of the particular needs
of the inhabitants.
Passages move around
and through buildings,
winding, weaving,
widening, cascading,
wandering in all directions.

"The true work of architecture

is not a monument, but a

receptacle of life, a construction

that lives close to its creator,

following him in the various,

fast changing functions of his

life, to each of which it lends a

certain form, a form that is never

finished or final, but that is

completed as time goes by,

flowering again and again into

daily perfection." Aris Konstantinidis

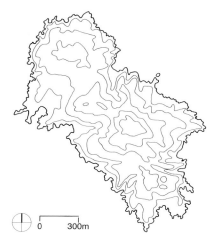

Like a pile of sugar cubes, whitewashed houses are densely clustered around two peaks topped with lonely chapels in Ios' main village of Khora. The individual parts may be simple, but the harmony and beauty of the whole is far more than a sum of parts. There is powerful order in the chaos, an overwhelmingly beautiful village that links the past and the future in the present. Ancient remains have been absorbed into the walls and streets and textures of Ios. Covered with oak forests centuries ago, the trees were used for building ships, leaving the island harsh and spectacularly rugged. Legend has it that Homer died here and was buried on the shore. The ebb and flow of life here changes with the seasons from tranquil to frenetic, old world Greek life side by side with young travelers, the haunting music of Theodorakis overlaid with the latest contemporary music. Languages from all over the world can be heard and with each new season new explorers arrive, new young minds who come face to face with a culture that has survived all onslaughts and continues to exist, strong on its foundations — foundations from which so many cultures sprang. Against the stark, mountainous terrain and the incredible beauty of the Aegean blue sky the village glows as though it is a dream, a memory of a past that is not ours but somehow becomes ours, because we have drunk in the magic and have become a part of this land, this land of Greece.

Ios

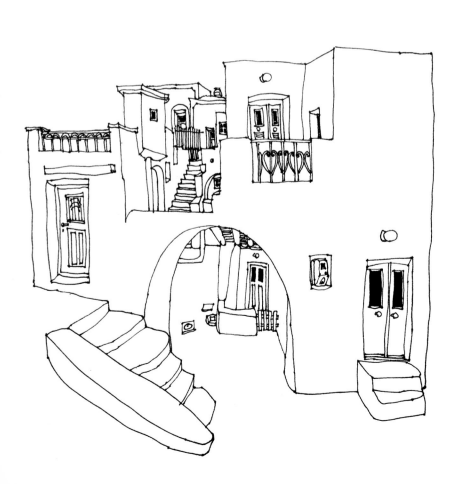

The first impression of simple cubic forms

dissolves instantly on entering

this complex and highly sculpted world.

The rugged site does not allow for

motorized movement

as every path is a set of stairs,

stairs that cascade, stairs that flow,

stairs that break through buildings

creating a tunnel, stairs leading

in all directions at the same time.

This is a place within which to glide

up, down, through, and around.

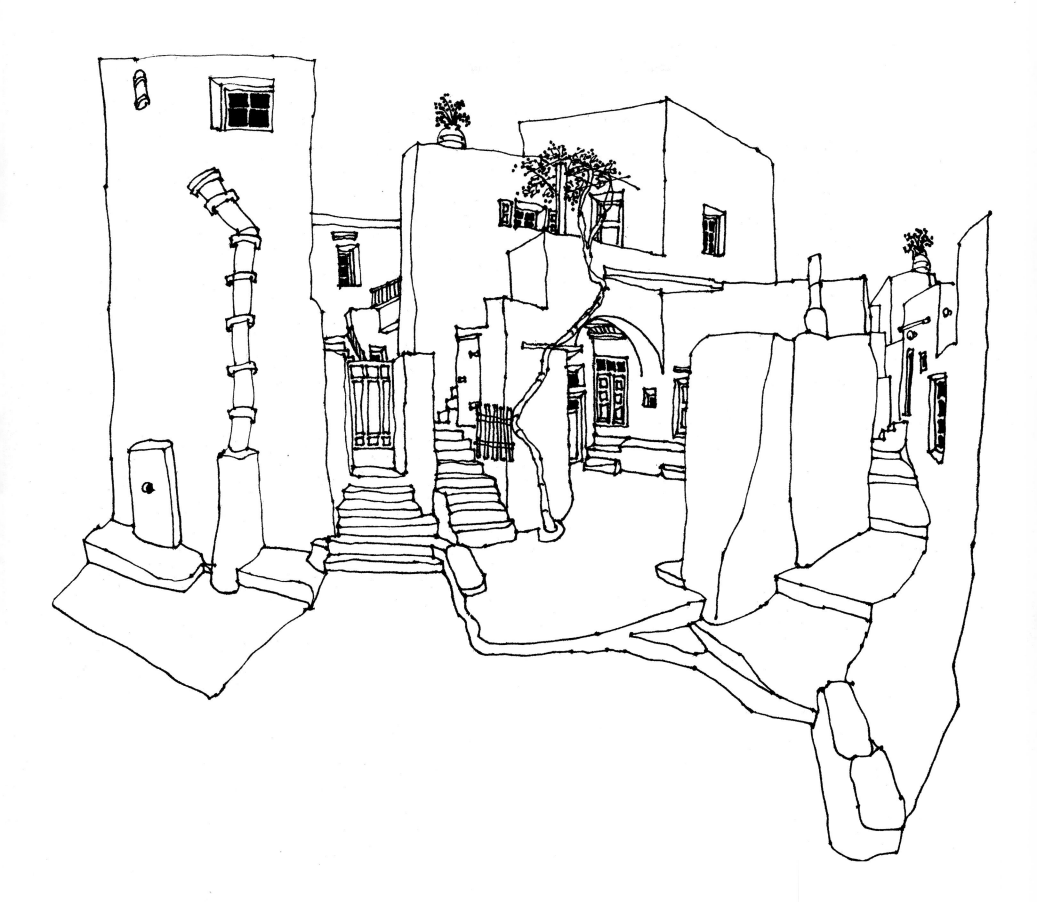

"What nobility and simplicity,
what a lack of rhetoric and pompousness.
Everything is cut to human proportions.
Never have grace and power merged as organically as they do here,
in this austere and smiling land of Greece." Kazantzakis

0   5km

Paros

Beautiful Paros, famed in antiquity for its translucent
marble, is more green than its neighboring islands with
fertile hillsides that slope gently to the sea. Occupied
since 3,000 BC by Mycenaeans, Ionians, Romans, and
Turks, the castles and grand churches have crumbled,
replaced by working windmills, fragrant lemon groves,
and tiny, unspoiled villages. Sprinkled like jewels on
gently rolling hills, these quaint villages are neatly
tucked into the embrace of a ravine and along the
shore with the deep-blue Aegean lapping at the legs of
cafe tables. Nausau, Lefkas, Marpissa — each has its
charms, all give abundantly of their magic... Wandering
along their pathways the vista changes with every
step...a soft curve, climb a few stairs, veer to the left, a
trellis offers dappled shade, a window shimmers with
the midday sun, a patio offers fragrant blossoms and
the sounds of children playing, a medieval archway
offers cool shade...this rich life is played out every day,
generation after generation.

A tiny stone house in the middle of a citrus grove in full
blossom was waiting just for us, our home for a while.
The fragrance of the blossoms was overwhelming and
the walk from the street to the house intoxicating.
Subtleties of detail abounded in unexpected places —
the shadows of the trellis tracing the sculpted forms of
the walls, dipping into niches as the sun ran its path
through the day, and in the only two sounds at night —
the waves washing the shore and the wind playing
among the blossoms...Slow, thyme-scented walks
filled our days, sketches filled our pages, and images
filled our cameras. It is no wonder that this was a
favorite haunt of poet, diplomat, and Nobel laureat
George Serefis. The air is thick with poetry, it enters
your very being with every breath.

164

"Pure forms will never bore us. Neither do we ever tire of nature. We have to learn from her to avoid overstatement and obviousness. We have to become aware of nature's subtlety and her fine surprises, and to translate these into our idiom. It is easy to invent the extravagant, the pretentious, and the exciting; but these are passing, leaving us only neurotic aimlessness. The things that have lasted and the things that will last are never subject to quick fashion. That good work and great work have been able to survive, we may take as a sign of the good sense in us, buried under temporary nonsense. Instead of adjusting our work to the public demand of the moment, let us direct it to this true sense of underlying value." Annie Albers

"A truly unprecedented and

advanced work is not that which

uses superficial brilliance to make

a temporary and sensationa

l impact, or that which seeks to

take one by surprise by means of

ostentatious, acrobatic

contortions, based on momentary

finds, but only by that which is

justified by a continuing, living

tradition, that which endures

because it is put to the test again

and again, within each new

context, so that it expresses

afresh inner experiences…forms

that have truly been handled over

and over again."

Aris Konstantinidis

The great wealth and prosperity of Sifnos that came from gold and silver mines and from stone quarries in days long past have given way to quiet windswept hillsides, rugged terrain, sandy beaches, and miles of dry stone walls meandering, terracing, dividing...The main village of Apolonia is a tight assemblage of walls, terraces, courtyards, and alleyways formed into a continuous complex of white cubes piled gently on three hills, stark and bold yet totally in harmony with the natural setting.

Mid winter there are few travelers and the inhabitants stay mostly indoors. We have the island to ourselves. Walking on the beach the air has a biting chill that the sun warms to comfortable. I notice small, terracotta pebbles moving gently with each wave, worn smooth. Closer examination reveals that they are not pebbles but shards of pottery, everywhere, thousands of them. They speak of time, of history, of life, and of death.

Perhaps they are from urns on an ancient vessel sunk long ago, broken, scattered by the currents, washing up here as the last remains from that distant time. In that distant past, someone harvested that clay from the earth, kneaded it to the right consistency, formed it with skilled hands into a shape suitable to its use. It might have been painted with decorations depicting daily life or something important in history, or maybe just a simple pattern and a signature, marking their work with pride. Those pots had to be well suited to their use to be chosen to serve on a ship. They would have been carefully loaded onto the vessel, filled and strapped into position for the journey. Was it a fierce battle, a raging storm that sent them to the bottom of the sea? What country were these pots from, where were they headed when all was lost? Were lives lost when these pots crumbled? Who cried for them? What of the treasure that might also have been on the ship? Who marked the existence of these people, the ship, these pots? Are they recorded in the annals of history or are these precious fragments all that remain?

Or, might these worn pieces speak of celebrations on this very beach, dancing and feasting? The beach is a beautiful place to gather, bathe in the deep-blue Aegean, cook a meal to share with friends and family. Perhaps the pots were broken in the frenzy of the dance and have simply been worn by time, water, and wind to these softly rounded pieces.

172

Whitewash, like the luminous skin of a living creature, breathes, glows, feels warm and soft to the touch. Brushed on twice a year, the thin, watery liquid dries to a powdery substance that is not a film like paint but a radiant, organic, weightless coating of light and of life. The honesty of the building forms, the brilliance of the light, the blueness of the sky and the ever-present sea — all are intensified by this whitewash, this washing on of whiteness, this cleansing and clarifying process of washing new life into the old.

three hundred and

sixty five chapels

dozens of dovecotes

and working windmills

scattered across the island

stark tiny constructions that

give scale and sparkle

to vast sweeps of gray land

"Architecture...is not only buildings, but all the works that man makes with his hands in the course of his daily occupations."

Heidegger

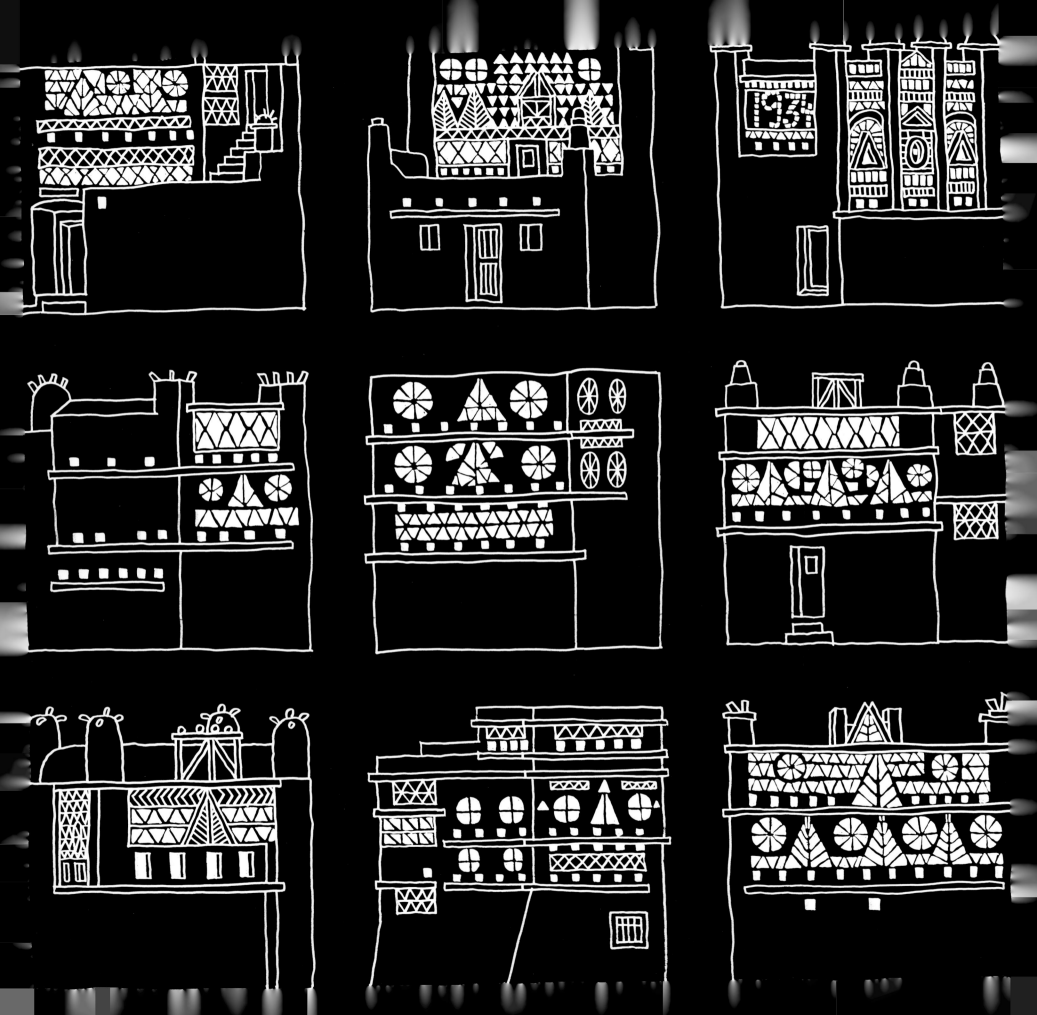

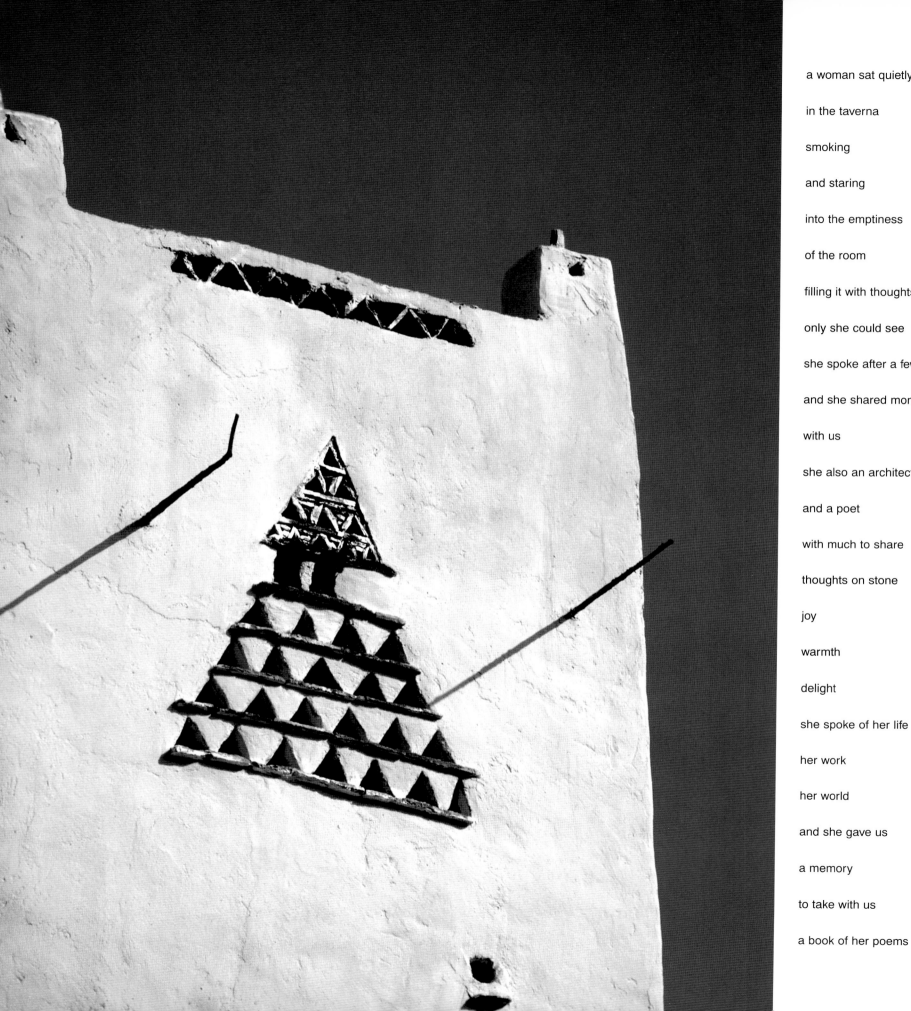

a woman sat quietly

in the taverna

smoking

and staring

into the emptiness

of the room

filling it with thoughts

only she could see

she spoke after a few days

and she shared moments of her life

with us

she also an architect

and a poet

with much to share

thoughts on stone

joy

warmth

delight

she spoke of her life

her work

her world

and she gave us

a memory

to take with us

a book of her poems

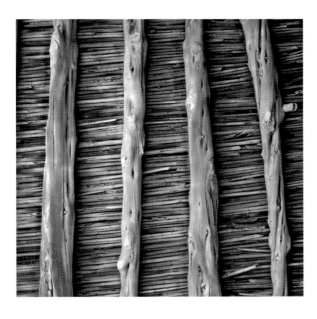

Mykonos

Fluid form sparkling in the sunlight, luminous as though lit from within, eroded by time and wind — whitewash sculpted into a spiritual mirage. Shadows clarify the details, a broken wall, a rough texture, a dark opening to the mysterious world within. The Paraportiani Church is a collection of four separate chapels melded together over the centuries into a sculpted mass of soft white form that is recognized as a national cultural treasure, monumental, yet unencumbered with classical responsibility. There is richness in the simplicity, harmony in the complexity, an overwhelming sense of appropriateness in this magic form that anchors Mykonos to the mythic world.

Mykonos is one of the more accessible Greek islands and, as such, has been burdened with the overwhelming onslaught of tourists. The main village is an excellent example of how beautiful places might protect themselves, in their growth and development to accommodate visitors, from destroying the very aspect that brings the visitors in the first place. Local building regulations carefully control the size, form, materials, and details of all new construction as well as prevent the destruction of existing structures of historical and cultural significance. This type of control has come too late for many extraordinary villages around the Mediterranean, but here on Mykonos they were implemented early enough and written well enough to do what they should. The result is a village that maintains its beauty and charm, despite the gold and sweater shops and the contemporary music blaring from every taverna. It is still possible to find original, organic architecture, and as a bonus, one can see how modern life can fit in a world designed for another age.

The harbor promenade

is the link between

the land and the sea,

between the village

and the rest of the world,

between yesterday and tomorrow.

The sea, an ever-present force

from which life sprang in the beginning

and from which life still springs.

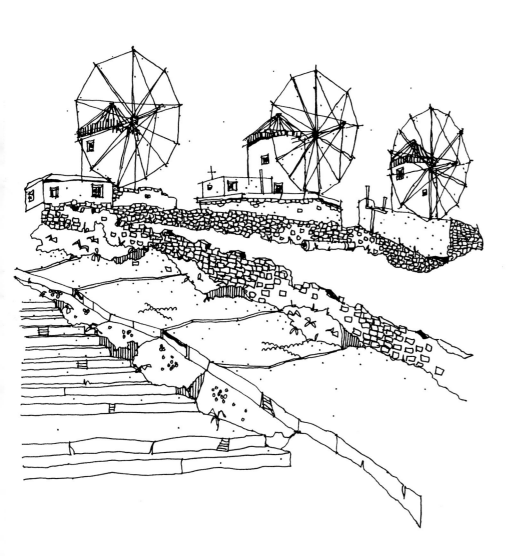

the street becomes

a tangled pattern

stairs weaving

into each other

breaking into

innumerable directions

the surprise of choice

heightening the richness

of movement

and of the moment

a journey can be

a straight path

moving from one place

to another

efficiently

or the journey

can be a dance

of discovery

allowing for visual

spiritual

and emotional

richness

in these villages

the journeys are

a dance of life

a dance so fluid

so unique

that it can not be repeated

that is new

each time it is danced

dazzling white houses
line a tangled maze
of twisting streets
a maze to foil invaders
in days gone by
now breaks the wind
into soft breezes
with each turn
a fascinating array
of stairs
balconies
terraces
anything that can
extend into the street
does
this profusion of elements
ablaze with potted plants
would be sensory overload
but for the
overwhelming calmness
that holds this chaos together
streets are narrow
and winding
often decorated
with whitewash
streaks of shadow
and sunlight
come from every direction

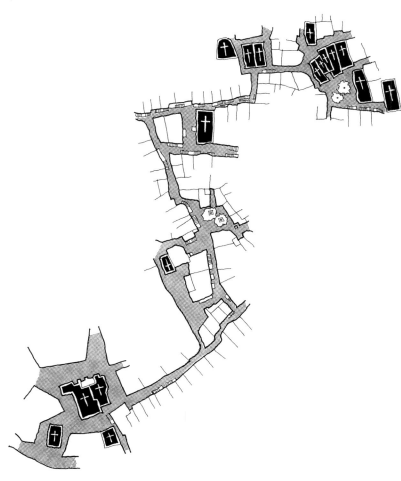

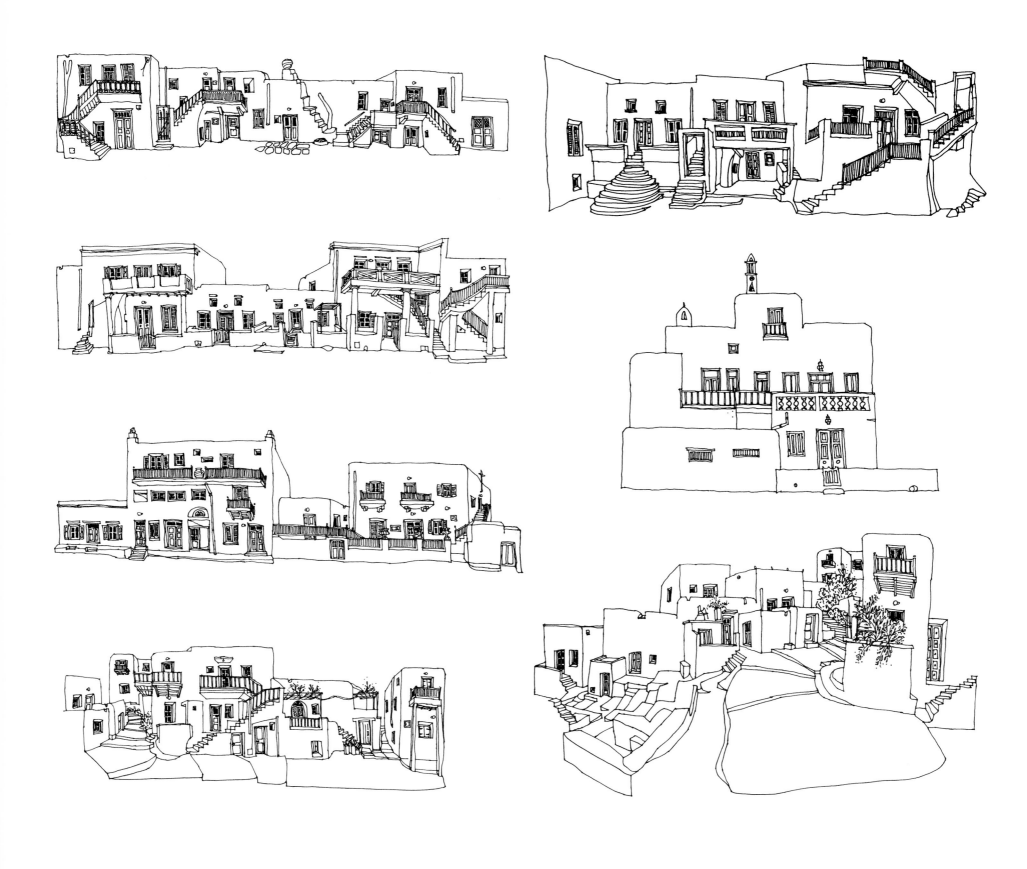

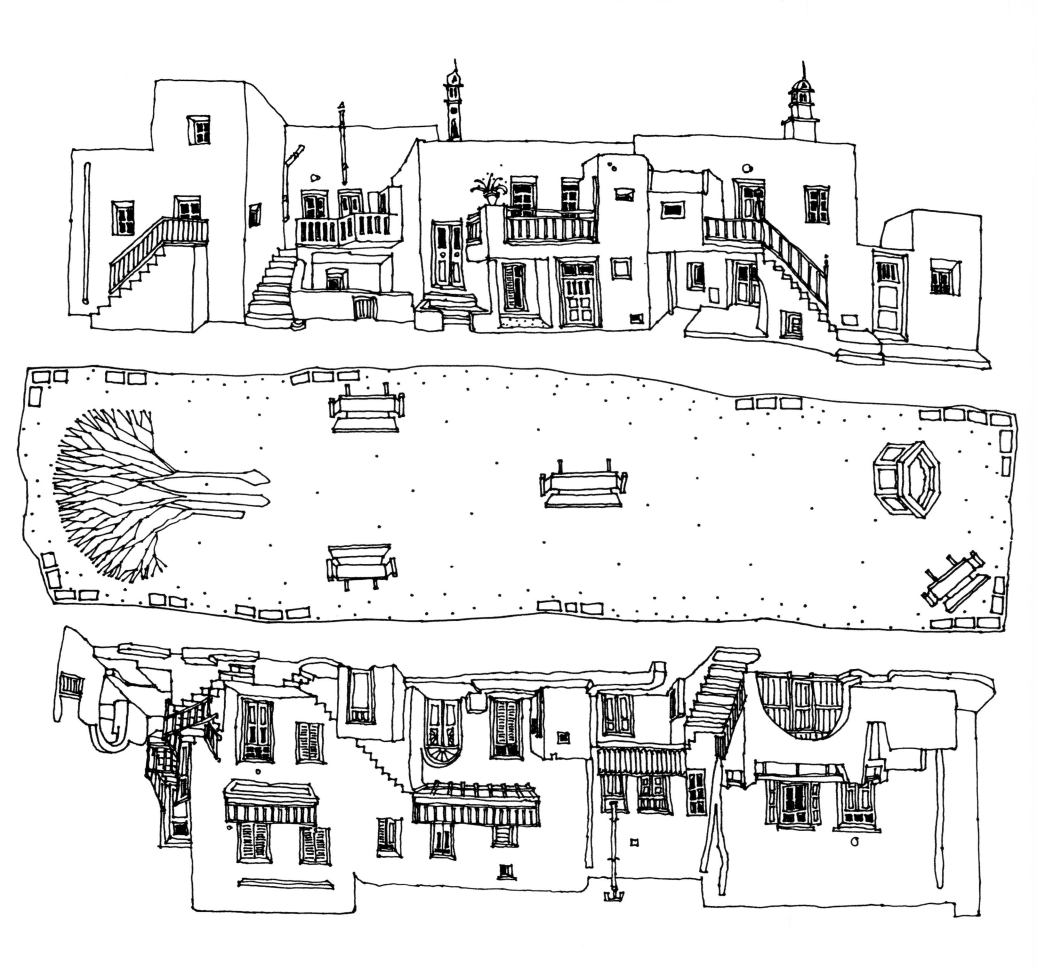

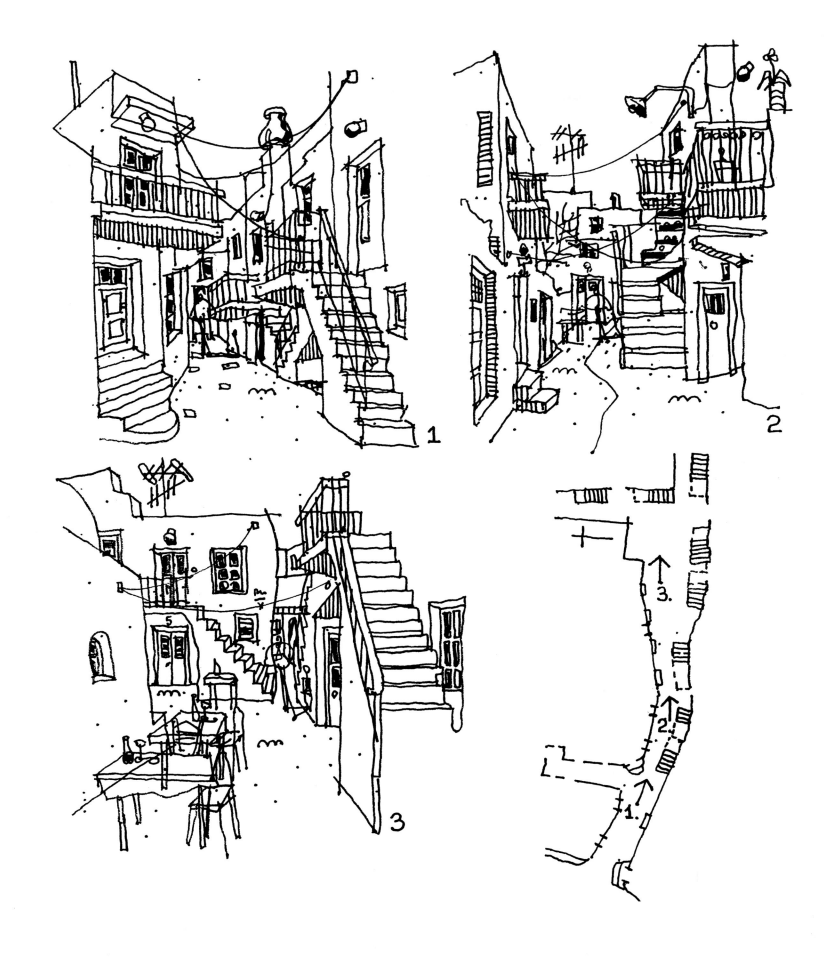

1

2

3

5

3.

2.

1.

"If nature had been comfortable, man never would have invented architecture." Oscar Wilde

"Love of life is nourished
and sustained,
one would think,
by the continuous motion
of the human hand
as it whitewashes,
day after day,
the walls and doorsteps
and window-sills of buildings.
And gradually,
day by day,
as each new coat of
whitewash covers the
previous one,
these surfaces
seem to acquire
a soft,
warm,
human-like skin;
you can lean against it
and touch it
and feel it breathing.
And how strange:
you often have the feeling
that these whitewashed
buildings
are not really constructions,
but living organisms
that have grown
out of human entrails,
in the same way
that a snail secretes its shell,
shaping its house
out of its own body."

Aris Konstantinidis

"Of all the people

the Greeks have dreamt

the dream of life

most beautifully."

Goethe

"When one has completed

the necessary,

the indispensable,

the useful,

one immediately

comes upon

the beautiful

and the pleasant."

Voltaire

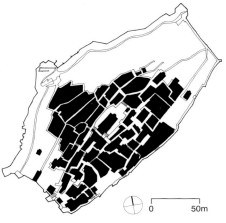

0   50m

Monemvasia

There is only one way into the fortified town of Monemvasia. Thus its name – only one entrance. Arrival here feels like reaching the edge of the world. The island was detached from the mainland by an ancient earthquake, reattached centuries later with the causeway which permits land access. Built into the base of a 984-foot/300-meter cliff on the Eastern coast of the Peloponnese, Monemvasia was an almost impregnable fortress, its inhabitants living a comfortable life, enjoying the fruits of trade and protected by its fleet. Monemvasia fell in 1249 only after a three-year siege. Cretan origins may be assumed from its ancient name of Minoa and Mycenaen ruins can still be seen. After their fall, Venetian, Papal, Byzantine, and Turkish rule each left its mark in the architecture of this magnificently situated town. A zigzag path leads up to the fortified upper town, mostly in ruins, a Byzantine castle preserved in Venetian form and the Church of Agia Sofia. The stones, whether still standing or laying scattered on the ground, carry their history in every facet. Venetian porticoes stand over fallen marble columns, a mosque niche graces one wall of a Byzantine church, monsters and fortress remnants protect frescoes of the birth of John the Baptist. The list alone of those who have passed through this strategically located, easily defended fortress stir with echoes of mythic places and heroic battles – Minoans, Venetians, Byzantines, Turks, Franks, Knights of Saint John. Now, the quiet, flower-filled lanes in the lower town show signs of life as the ruins are being carefully restored into new homes and a new town.

202

"The men who love and respect
and worship their art,
as the most precious thing in life,
and identify themselves
with the events they describe,
are the ones who seek
and find in each tradition,
even the most ancient,
that which they wish
to achieve themselves,
in their own time,
with their own faith and vision."

Solomos

"A village standing out sharply on the steep slope of a mountain, forming a collective facade, as the houses are grouped very close together or on top of each other, is a clear example of the unity of spirit, the unity of style achieved in true architecture. It is achieved, not only because the same local materials were used, but because all the houses were brought into being by common life requirements, out of a single will relating all of the village people in a common effort. This is what gives the buildings a similar aspect, a similar character, a kindred soul and look. In the same way, the people who built these houses belong to an organically related social entity, retaining a common spirit in the rhythm of their lives." Aris Konstantinidis

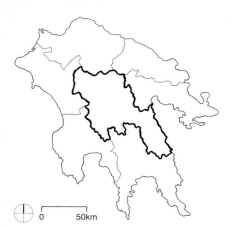

0 50km

Arcadia

Known since ancient times as the island of Pelops, or Peloponnese, this southernmost part of the mainland of Greece was actually a peninsula, until it was breached by the Corinth Canal and became an island. Myth has it that Pelops, son of Tantalos, was served to his father by the Gods as food and the Olympic games were founded at his funeral to honor his memory. This vast, mountainous land has high mountain peaks, remote forests, deep gorges, and is home to quiet villages, ancient ruins, and beautiful countryside. Haunting imagery of ancient Greece springs to mind from the names of so many historic and mythic places dotting this region – Epidaurous, Mycenae, Mistra, Sparta, Corinth, Olympia. In the midst of these places, in the middle of the Peloponnese, lies the mountainous region of Arcadia.

Deep in the center of Arcadia, the hill towns of Andritsena, Dimitsana, and Stiminitsa exist now much as they have for centuries. Showing evidence of occupation since pre-history, this area is so remote that wars rarely touched it and the inhabitants did not develop the city-state, as did, for example, Athens and Sparta. Ancient Cyclopian walls stand side by side with Frankish and Norman details. Dimitsana, long a center of learning, played a key role in the War of Independence. Steminitsa, also known as Ipsounda, nestled into wooded slopes cut by deep ravines, was known for its iron craftsmanship. Andritsana was and still is a market town and, like Dimitsana and Steminitsa, though they were cut off from the rest of Greece, developed trade with distant lands. Beautiful handmade red tile roofs complement the rustic wooden constructions and the projecting upper balconies. Recent improvements in the road system have made access into this rugged area only a little easier. Red roof tiles and projecting second-floor wooden balconies are unique in Andritsena. Quiet, cobblestone lanes, the sounds of chickens, dogs, and children at play, music, and the aroma from kitchens carried on the breeze...in these villages magic exists that allow one to step back in time without the aid of a time machine.

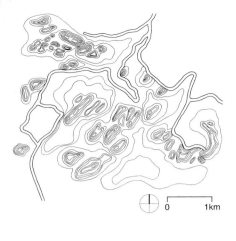

0   1km

Meteora

216

Massive pinnacles of gray rock rise from the Thessalian plain, lifting their sacred holdings toward the heavens. These fantastic columns of limestone, some as high as 984 feet/300 meters above the surrounding plain, still stand after centuries of water from the Peneios river and its tributaries washed away the softer stone. Meteora meaning "in the air" became the name for the cenobitic monasteries perched atop these towering refuges. Hermits first sought solitude in the caves of these Meteora in the 11th century, and in the 14th century with invaders from all sides, the monks began to group together to form the monasteries in the most inaccessible sites. Over the next centuries the number of monasteries increased to twenty-four, graced with holy icons and frescoes by great artists of the day. Only four of these great structures remain inhabited and the former rope ladders have been replaced with steps carved into the rock faces to allow visitors.

We found Meteora shrouded in fog and freezing mist. Billowing clouds of damp, cold air swirled around us, cutting visibility to zero then parting enough to reveal a towering mass right there in front of us. Seeing these mystical forms fade in and out of view, feeling completely disoriented by the play of light and shadow on structures not connected to, or even of this world, seemed a more appropriate experience than seeing them in the light of day. The sounds of the fog, the smell of the rock, the darkness of the light, the transparency of the shadow...all senses heightened, and confused...ethereal.

"The Greek light,

that gives such a

brilliant aspect

to every

constructed surface;

the Greek light,

that transparent,

weightless light,

full of spirit –

that clothes and

unclothes all things."

Kazantzakis

Dalmatia

Slovenia

□ Zagreb

Piran

Rovinj

Croatia

Bosnia and
Herzegovina

Zadar

□ Belgrade

Serbia and
Montenegro

□ Sarajevo

Trogir

□ Split

Mostar

Dubrovnik

□ Skopje

The Former Yugoslav
Republic of Macedonia

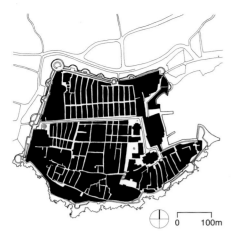

Dubrovnik

Embraced within massive fortress walls in a magnificent setting on the south Adriatic coast, Dubrovnik is an exquisitely preserved Renaissance city with a rich past and cultural heritage. Taking its name from the Slav word "dubrova", meaning oak forest, much of its architectural style came from the Venetians who occupied the city from 1205 to 1358. An independent republic for centuries, crafts and the arts flourished. Far-reaching trade developed a skillful merchant class who, along with the City's diplomats, managed to protect Dubrovnik from invasion and plundering, the unfortunate fate of so many beautiful cities along this coast.

Majestic, ancient ramparts, massive fortress walls, embrace, protect, divide, separate. They contain and repel, undulating with the terrain, a harmonious reflection of the beauty of nature. The walk along the ramparts, originally for the watch, is now a promenade, high, looking across, over, down, beyond, an aerial view of life as it goes on, day after day. The stone of Dubrovnik is unique. It has a color, a luminosity, that, once seen, cannot be forgotten. It is not that it "looks" different than other stone, its "look" penetrates beyond vision, it enters deeper than the realm of vision. As the sun traces its patterns across the sky, the days, the hours, the minutes, are recorded by every stone. Glinting in the morning light, they greet each new day with sharp clarity. Long shadows midday, cast by the choice of the stone cutter's hand who so long ago chipped and shaped every inch, soften mid afternoon to hide the scars and, as evening approaches and the air cools, the wall, the stones, share the warmth they gather during the day with us as we watch the sunset, our jackets in our room.

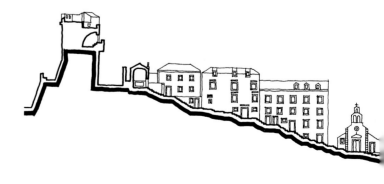

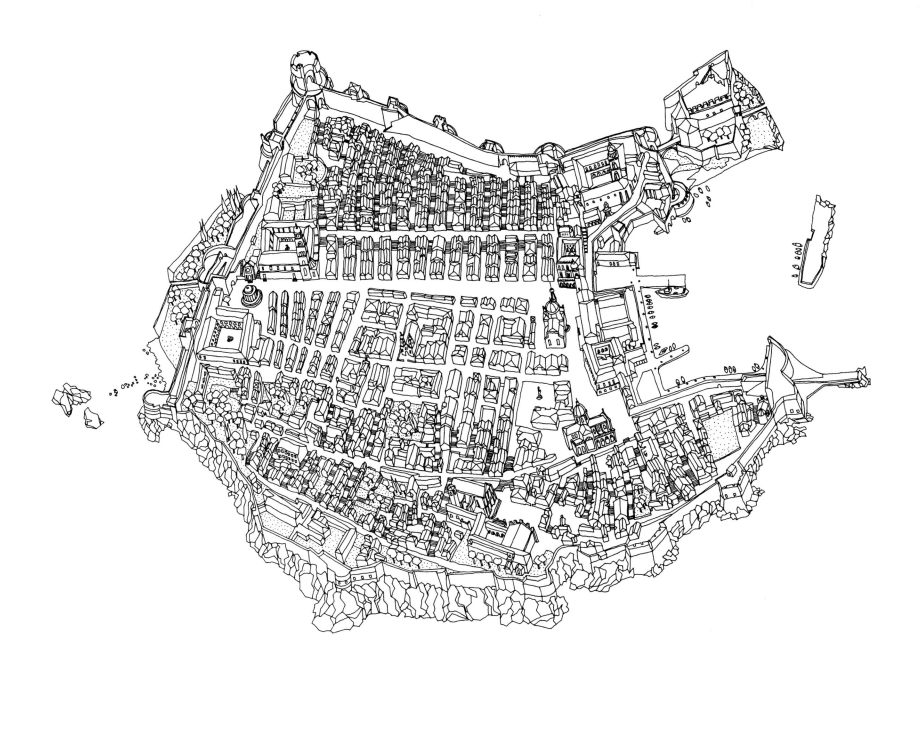
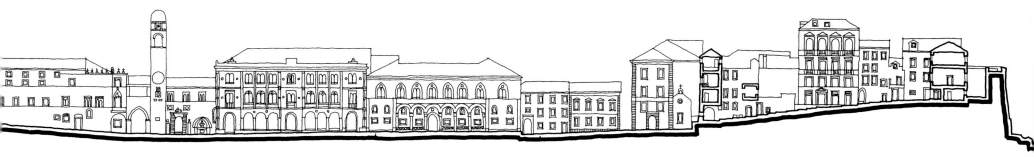

This elevated walk along these walls
offers a different perspective.
Roofs layer against each other, against the sea,
rather than against the sky.
Looking down on the life of the city
clarifies the spirit of the place.
Seeing, but not being in the midst of the activities,
emphasizes patterns, pauses, movement, shadows.
Textured roofs show the marks of their history in the moss,
mold and shifted lines that reflect earthquakes, war, repair.
The stone walls, each stone hand cut and carefully placed,
stand strong in their capacity of protector.

Placa, Dubrovnik's main street,

is more like a long, narrow plaza,

alive with activity.

Once a canal, long ago filled

and paved with stone

that is so polished

it feels soft to the touch.

Steep side streets

pour their living fluid

down and through Placa,

through plaza after plaza,

nourishing all of the public spaces

with a natural flow of human life.

This is a place of pedestrians.

Every step reveals new compositions

in windows, doors, moldings,

a stimulating and inspirational dialogue

with the past and the present,

every encounter a memory to keep.

A natural perfume of the sea

and lemons pervade every lane.

No detail in Dubrovnik competes

for individual attention.

Each offers its modest beauty

as an integral part

of the whole that is this

unique and harmonious city.

Placa

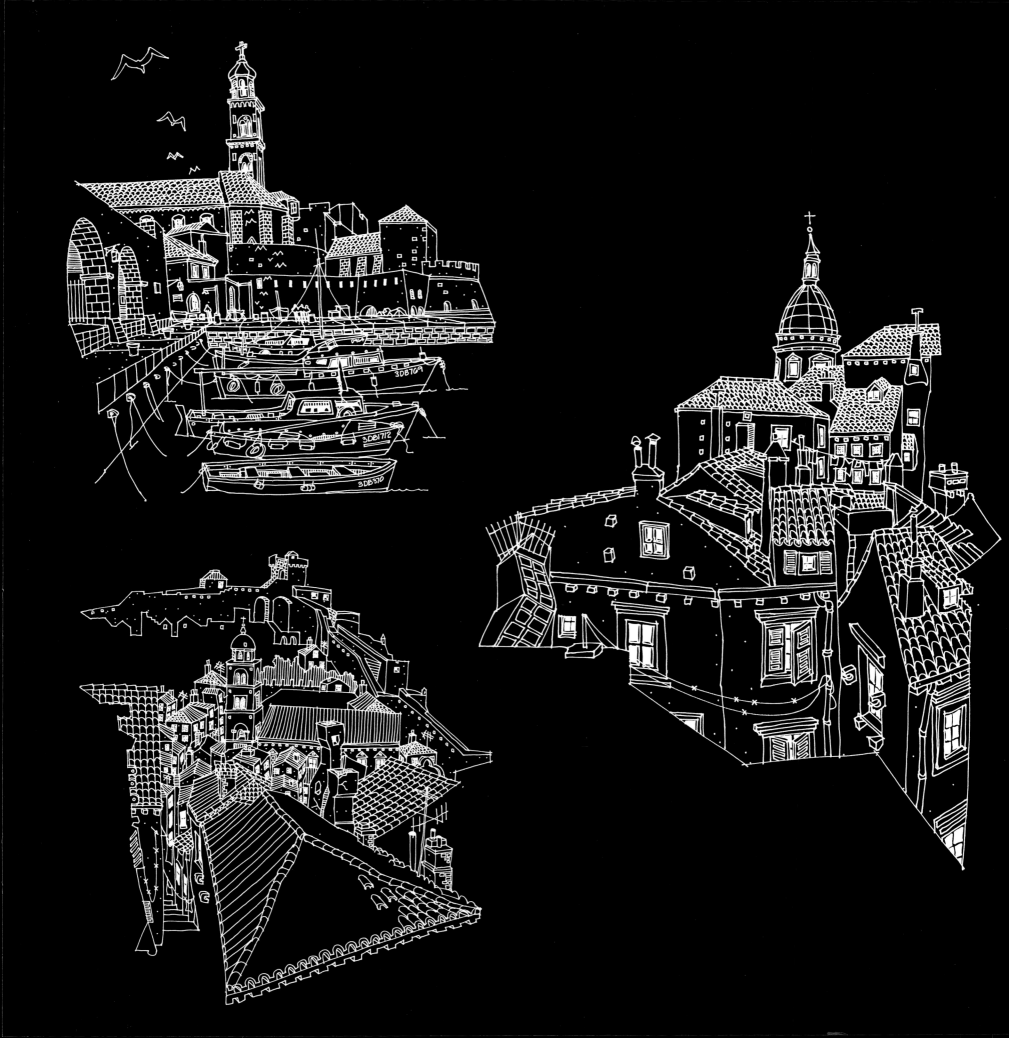

an old vase on the table in our room, chipped the table scratched the room thick walled lace curtains at the windows looking closer at the vase, hand thrown, hand painted, sits slightly tilted, the table, hand carved, beautiful joinery the room, cool in the summer hand made adobe bricks lace curtains, hand knotted, hand sewn, casting moving patterns on the wall, the vase, generations old, holding flowers picked this morning from the garden outside the window the window, hand carved, ancient glass, wavy with bubbles, distorting the view to the flower garden into a living Monet the breeze playing in the garden carries soft fragrance through the window, gently moving the curtain, scattering sprinkles of light on the wall, its surface irregular to the touch, from the hands that formed it, that plastered it, that painted it we are enveloped in a web of light, texture, fragrance, movement, history every hand that made these objects now embraces us, sharing their tenderness, their caress, sweet with gentle reminders of where we are and how long the journey to this day

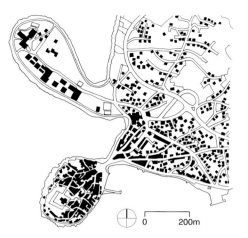

0   200m

Primosten

An island, an islet really, a village rising from the sea, completely covering the land from which it springs. This tiny town and harbor between the coves of Raduca and Primosten was connected in the 16th century to the mainland by a causeway that, though it physically ties this village to the body of the continent, has not connected this beautiful place to the here and now. With an economy based on farming, vineyards, and olives, and on fishing, the bridge connected the islanders to their farms but left their homes to linger in peace, apart from the advances of time and change. There is a curious sense of both serenity and confusion – crisp order in chaos...in the sharp forms of the buildings made from rough stone walls and roofs, formed in the most primitive of manners. Stones lay flat, one overlapping the next – protecting and repelling... protecting the inhabitants and their ways of life, repelling oppressors and those who would destroy that way of life – protecting tradition, repelling the new world.

Each element stands strong in its

function – shingles of stone glisten with

sharp shadow in random patterns of a

clear-cut whole. Shutters barely open

invite the question of what lies behind.

morning light sparkling on roof stones

that which is solid becomes translucent

that which is roughly textured softly glistens

sunlight can reveal all detail or can

strip away all detail to reveal the essence

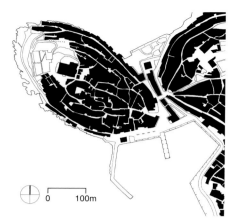

0   100m

Rovinj

Rovinj is a sparkling jewel floating in the Adriatic Sea - a village which completely covers the island on which it stands. Though connected to the mainland, Rovinj is distinct in form and remains in tact as a separate entity. Narrow stone passages between tightly clustered houses invite surprise at every turn. Fishermen discuss the day's catch as children play among their brightly colored nets along the promenade that ties this land to the sea. Modeled after the campanile of San Marco in Venice, the tower and church at the crest of the hill is always visible. Fragments of days gone by - a Roman crypt, a Venetian molding, an ancient gateway - tell the stories of many centuries. A mother's call to her children echoes now as it always has, here in this magic place. In these villages time stands still and yet it marches on. An ancient wall contains a new cinema. Poetry written deep in the past captures a moment from yesterday. Time unfolds every day, marking its passage in the rhythms of the sun, the gardens, the seasons, the laughter of children, the celebrations of birth and of death. The sea is ever present, embracing, invading, surrounding, breathing. Every vista begins and ends at the sea. Sky and water, each blue, sometimes distinct, sometimes melded. Where the sky ends the sea begins; where the sea ends the sky begins. Caught in this magic space between the sky and the sea, these stones tell stories of centuries, of generations, of wars, of loves. They are warm on cold nights and cool on hot afternoons. The stones know all but do not tell - they leave room for your own imaginings.

242

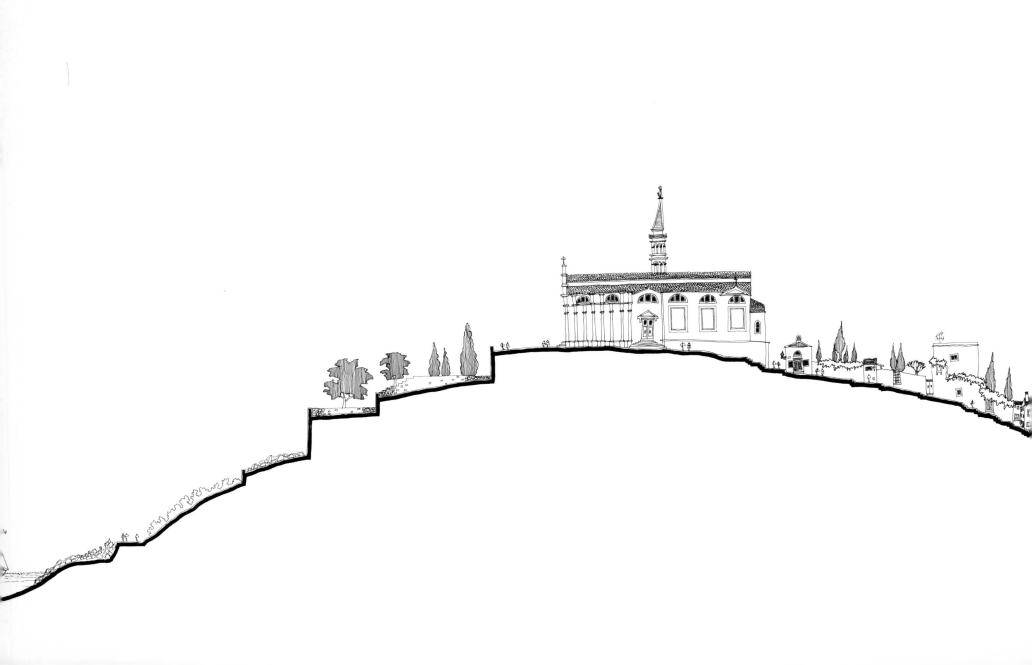

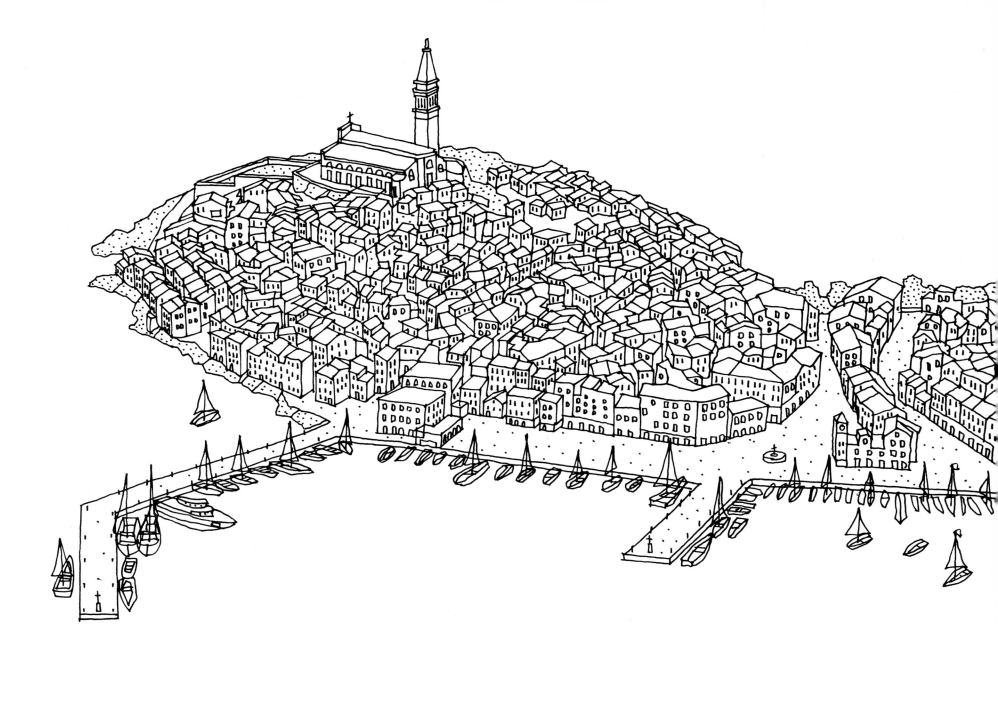

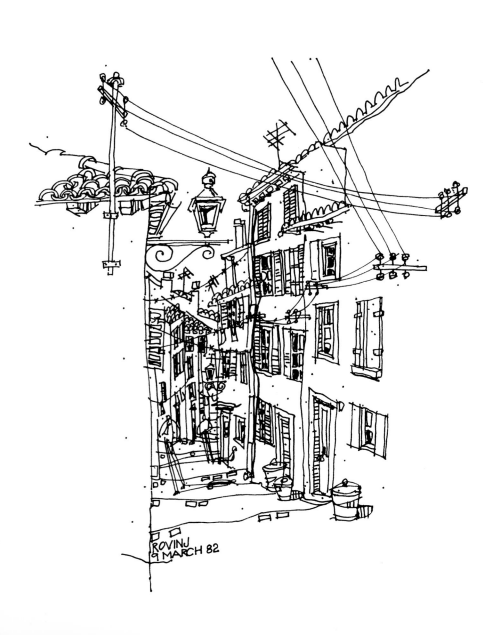

ROVINJ
9 MARCH 82

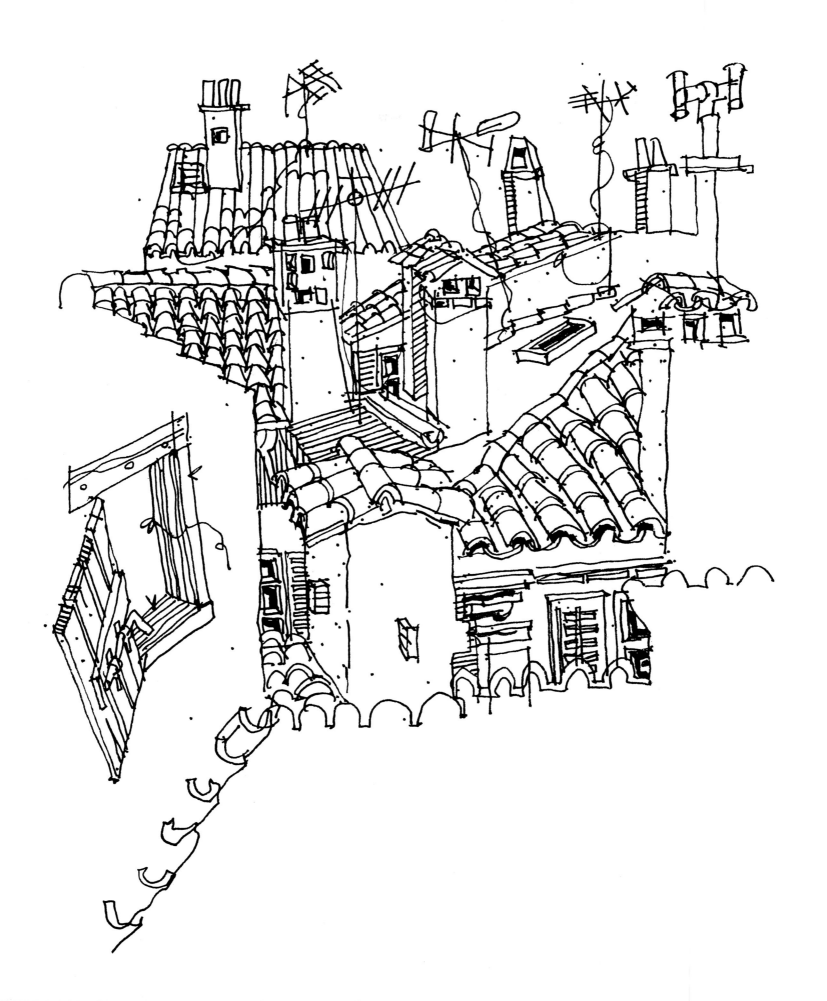

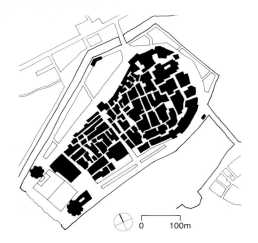

0   100m

Trogir

An islet off the Dalmatian Coast, Trogir is a self-contained, living museum, an island fortified against the world, sharing and yet protecting traces of all those who have passed through. Fresh fruits and flowers, homemade cheeses, shoes, tools, clothes – all the essentials of life can be found at the daily market woven among a harmonious collection of Gothic, Romanesque, Venetian, Byzantine, Dalmatian, Greek, and Renaissance architectural masterpieces. In 1997 Trogir was added to the UNESCO World Heritage List. Decayed relics stand side by side with living memories. Sounds of the stone cutters echo in the cobbled streets. Carpenters plane new wood into shutters to fit within ancient openings. Centuries-old roof tiles are carefully collected from a ruin to be used again and again, blurring the lines between old and new, past and present. Lives pass through the market. Children grow old and generations come and go, but the market remains, feeding the inhabitants. The market is a stage where the play of life repeats and repeats – always the same, never the same, different players over the centuries, the same needs being met in this market of life.

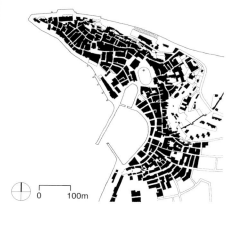

On the northern coast of the Istrian Peninsula, a finger of land reaches out into the Adriatic Sea toward Venice and Trieste, toward the worlds that conquered and left their traces in the towers and moldings – Greeks and Byzantines, French and Franks, Austrians and Venetians. Pirates fortified the town with massive walls that now offer spectacular views over the town and the harbor to the Adriatic and Italy beyond. Piran is laced with a maze of narrow cobbled lanes – each a different, beautiful journey to the same place. To wander here is a delight, to discover the same place in so many ways.

A world within a world within a world within a world...There is a layering of space and an encircling of form that is tangible but not visible. A chair at a cafe table contained by tables on three sides, within a cafe contained by plants on three sides, within the plaza contained by buildings on three sides, open to the harbor contained by the promenade on three sides, open to the Adriatic Sea contained by Venice and Trieste and Piran on three sides...Space that is defined yet undefined, there to feel or to ignore. Sitting at the table within the cafe within the plaza within the town, open to the harbor and the promenade, open to the Adriatic Sea, open to the Mediterranean, open to the Atlantic Ocean, touching the shores of Africa and America and Brazil and the Pacific Ocean and Asia....where are boundaries...how is space really defined? Is the invisible line tangible, do all spaces touch all spaces? How do you know where you are? Sitting at the table in the cafe there is an embrace, you are safe, with only a plant separating you from all the world as you sit there with your cup of coffee and a

254

The walls of our room are a bright aqua color with a
repetitive floral pattern. At first glance it appears to be
wallpaper, garish in color, with a primitive, plain little
print. Laying in bed in the morning looking at the walls
a little closer, we realize that it is not wallpaper, but
hand painted and printed with what could have been a
potato stamp, repetitive but irregular, the lines
distorting as the hand applying the pattern grew tired
or reached a little too far. The aqua color, cheery at
sunrise, suddenly seems cool on the hot afternoon,
soft and welcoming at the end of the day. First, quick,
judgments fail when the subject is given time to
express itself, fail when we take time to contemplate
what we are seeing, fail when we realize that we are
enriched by their embrace.

The buildings around the plaza

form a circular embrace.

The curving streets

hold tight

to the buildings.

It is easy to become lost

within these winding streets

yet there is

a sense of anticipation

rather than wariness,

a sense of security

rather than fear.

What is not yet seen

is a delight

awaiting discovery.

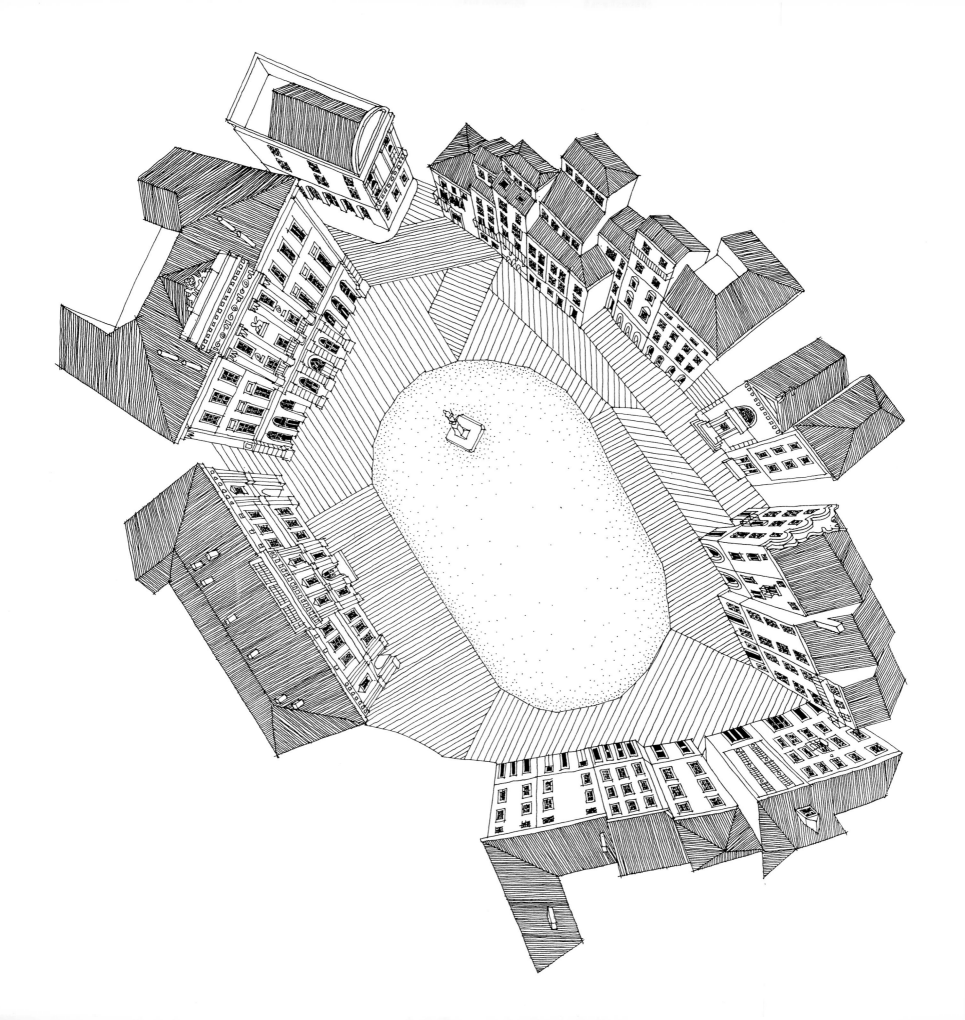

"The true basis for any serious study of the area of Architecture still lies in those indigenous, more humble buildings everywhere that are to architecture what folklore is to literature or folksong is to music and with which academic architects are seldom concerned. Though often slight, their virtue is intimately related to the environment and to the heartlife of the people. Functions are truthfully conceived and rendered with natural feeling. Results are often beautiful and always constructive." Frank Lloyd Wright

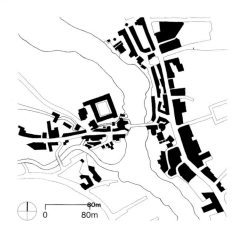

Mostar was one of the loveliest and most distinctive cities in this part of the world. Was, because it has lost an architectural world treasure that gave it beauty and distinction – its extraordinary, ancient bridge. The name of this place comes from its bridge. "Most" – meaning bridge, and "Stari" – meaning old. Most-stari – now Mostar. In this dramatic gorge in the heart of the Neretva River canyon, a community began around an old wooden Roman bridge. The Sultan Suleiman the Magnificent commissioned Mimar Hairedin, a Turkish engineer, to create a single span stone bridge, which was completed in 1566 after nine years of construction. Legend has it that the Sultan vowed to execute the engineer if the bridge should fail. Hairedin disappeared on the day the supports were removed and was found some time later digging his own grave. This "fossilized crescent", as it was also known, stood for 427 years, a graceful stone arch spanning almost a hundred feet and regarded as a masterpiece of Turkish engineering and elegance.

The fate of this land may have been determined as far back as the 4th century when a line drawn on a map through this area divided the Roman Empire into east and west, and throughout the centuries it became the division between the Frankish and Byzantine empires, between the Catholic and Orthodox churches, between the Christian West and the Islamic East, and now is on the dividing line between Croatia and Bosnia-Herzegovina.

When crowds gathered to watch us sketch and excitedly pointed out whose home each was, it did not matter then if one was Serb and the other Croatian, one Christian and the other Muslim. They were a community who knew each other; they stood around us as a group and named their differences, named them with laughter and with pride. How did it come to pass that this beautiful river divided this community, each to its own side, and that this bridge became the last link connecting them, destroyed on November 9th, 1993, shelled out of existence by a tank? This was a treasure so special that its loss is a loss to the whole world, not just to those who let it divide them and then destroyed it. I cried on the day this bridge fell, cried for the bridge, cried for the sadness of their fight, cried for all those who will not see the beauty we found when we ventured into their world.

Mostar

Cross stones reaching
from side to side,
raised to provide
a foothold for each step.
The incline so steep
that feet must be carefully placed,
the rise such that
the other side is a mystery
until your eyes reach the crest.
Stones worn smooth,
polished by centuries of feet,
inhabitants passing
from one side to the other,
travelers passing
from one region to another,
polished by life,
destroyed by death.
We mourn this bridge
and what the inhabitants
and the world
have lost
by its fall.

Spain

Barcelona □

□ Madrid

■ Cuenca

□ Lisbon

Valencia □

□ Cordoba

■ Quesada

□ Seville

Montefrio ■   ■ Guadix

□ Granada

■ Setenil

Casares ■

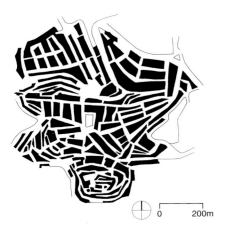

0   200m

Quesada

The town of Quesada is a compact, tightly curved form beautifully situated against a backdrop of rugged mountains. The embracing curve of the protective outer walls, originating as a defense, now adds a serene calm to a quiet place where chattering birds are the only invaders. Remnants of Moorish occupation can be found in the ancient walls and intricate detailing. Wide streets tightly lined with whitewashed houses spiral up the hill, crowned with the church. As is typical in so many Spanish towns, the streets are full of people and activity. The parallel walls of the unarticulated house facades amplify street sounds to a deafening level. This is characteristic of many Andalusian towns, and in sharp contrast to their otherwise peaceful nature.

We discovered Quesada while exploring this region and, because we have a friend of the same name, decided to stay awhile. A little room in the center of town with a balcony overlooking the main square became our home and our generous hostess graciously hand-washed our clothes and hung them to dry on her roof in the fragrant breezes. Exploration around town led to an old woman with keys to the local art museum, a beautiful building, a proud collection of paintings honoring one of Spain's great contemporary artists, Rafael Zabaleta, born and revered here, his hometown. There is always joy in being surprised by the unexpected. To find bold, passionate paintings celebrated with such pride by the inhabitants of this tiny, remote village invited a sense of awe and joy in us and serves still as an inspiration that wonder still abounds all around us, sometimes in the most unexpected places.

270

Looking over the tawny texture of the roofs, there is a sense of tranquility that these beautiful handmade tiles bring to the chaos of forms. Ideas of conformity and individuality, traditional and contemporary, come into question when quietly contemplating these beautiful villages. Houses are similar yet unique, forms are compatible with each other, yet each responds to the needs of the owner and to the specific dictates of the sun and wind for their location. Each region uses similar forms and materials in their buildings, but there is no forced repetition or application of arbitrary ornamentation for the sake of "style." This truly traditional architectural typology develops in an organic manner, form that evolves from a richness of life, of culture. Materials are similar because they are "of their place," locally available, and serve well the task to which they are put. Scale develops from a respectful appreciation of appropriate size. Arrangement of buildings relative to each other is carefully considered.

"Material which was derived from

light was spent light. Spent light

was a material which cast a

shadow by the grace of light, and

the shadows belonged to the light."

Louis Kahn

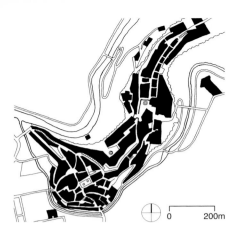

0   200m

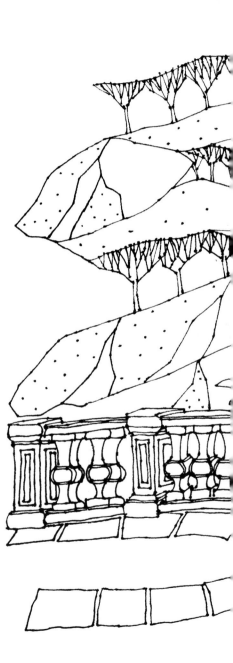

Cuenca

The ancient town of Cuenca hangs in an impregnable position on the Serrania de Cuenca surrounded on three sides by cliffs that plunge into the deep valleys of the Huecar and the Jucar rivers. This hilly, boulder strewn region east of Madrid has been home to Romans, Visigoths, and Moors, each of whom left their marks in the grand mansions with their coats of arms, in the textures of the stone walls and in the steep, medieval cobbled streets lined with Baroque and Gothic churches. The spectacular gorge that separates Cuenca from the rest of the world is spanned by eight old bridges, and, though they give passage, they have not allowed the modern world to intrude. As one of UNESCO's World Heritage Sites, Cuenca is recognized as an extraordinarily rich architectural and cultural treasure. With limited land, the homes were built tall and narrow. Cuenca's Casas Colgadas or hanging houses, seem to be almost natural extensions of the cliff walls, some looking like ancient high-rises. Gracious homes tower on the precipitous cliffs with wooden balconies and wrought iron grilles hanging like multitiered jewelry. A stillness rises from the deep canyons and invades every corner of Cuenca, even in the sounds of children, cars and dogs echoing softly against the stone walls.

CUENCA
SPAIN

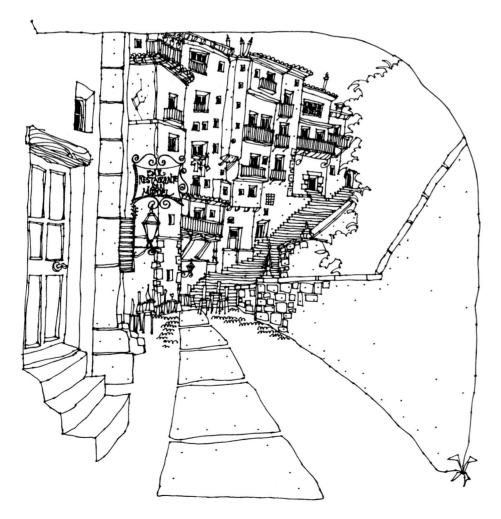

"Being faithful to a style...does not mean the reverent reproduction of other people's creation. It is not enough to copy even the very best buildings of another generation or another locality. The method of building may be used, but you must strip from this method all the substance of particular character and detail, and drive out from your mind the picture of the houses that so beautifully fulfilled your desires. You must start right from the beginning, letting the new building grow from the daily lives of the people who will live in them, shaping the houses to the measure of the people's songs, weaving the patterns of a village as if on the village looms, mindful of the trees and the crops that will grow there, respectful of the skyline and humble before the seasons. There must be neither faked tradition nor faked modernity, but an architecture that will be the visible and permanent expression of the character of a community. This would mean nothing less than a whole new architecture." Hassan Fathy

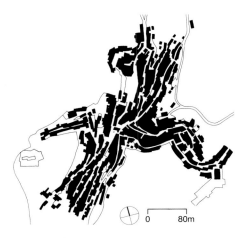

0   80m

Casares

Scattered across three hills like a handful of building blocks, the sparkling white town of Casares is one of those places that looks too beautiful to be real. Gently curving streets lined with tightly packed houses twist and turn their way up and around. Sunlight spills into every corner at some point during the day, breezes dance through the streets. An ancient castle and an old cemetery crown one of the hills, laying the dearly departed as close to heaven as possible. The basic cubic form of the houses and the honeycomb vaults of the burial crypts speak of an organic, "form-follows-function" attitude. Beauty can truly be found in the simplest response to basic needs.

There are no spectacular mansions, no palatial details, nothing grandiose, just simple cubic forms of unpretentious homes – yet the sum of these little parts is an overwhelmingly rich architectural experience. Just meandering along the narrow streets and paths the experience takes new dimension every few steps – views open and surprise awaits at every turn. Tiny plazas invite gathering but, as in most Spanish towns, the street is the most important social space.

286

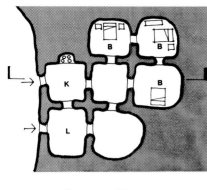

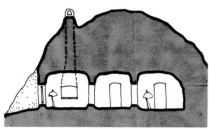

Guadix

In a region that can be extremely inhospitable, hollowing into the earth can have many advantages, not the least of which is cool shelter. East of Granada in the heart of Andalucia, an unearthly landscape of ragged land, severely eroded and baked under broiling sun, has offered civilized shelter since prehistoric times. Dusty roads meander through bleak desolation where a whitewashed swath on a cliff wall identifies a door to life hollowed into the earth. Chimneys and antennas sprout from jagged mounds. Inside the caves of Guadix, shady coolness is pierced with shafts of light from above and the sounds of music and "telenovelas" seep through the earth to mix with those of chickens and dogs.

Though so many of the villages throughout the Mediterranean are beautiful examples of vernacular architecture, architecture of its place, responsive to its environment, few are so bold as Guadix in representing intelligent solutions to adverse conditions. Why people would actually choose to settle in such an inhospitable region is certainly a question, but how they have dealt with the realities of that choice offers much to ponder. With no mechanical assistance, nothing of modern technology, the inhabitants of Guadix are quite comfortable in their homes. Sitting on the covered terrace of our hotel room in the newer, more conventional section of town nearby, neither the shade nor the curtains at the windows, not even the electric fan offered greater comfort than the cool earth of the caves nearby.

292

"Though thirty spokes may form the wheel

it is the hole within the hub

which gives the wheel utility.

It is not the clay the potter throws,

which gives the pot its usefulness,

but the space within the shape,

from which the pot is made.

Without a door, the room cannot be entered,

and without windows, it is dark."

Paolo Portoghesi

"The artist is a receptacle for

emotions, regardless of whether they

spring from heaven from earth, from

a scrap of paper, from a passing

face, or from a spider's web."

Picasso

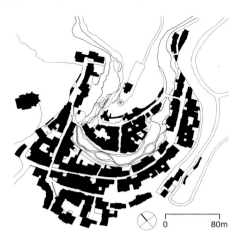

0   80m

Setenil

Much of the landscape in southern Spain is harsh and rugged. Brown land dotted with silvery gray olive trees, rocky gorges and steep cliffs give way only begrudgingly to the beautiful villages and towns. Even still, there is a sense of serenity in these villages, in their fluid, interdependent harmony with the specifics of the land they occupy, almost as though they are truly a part of each other. In this rolling countryside, the gentle persistence of the Guadalporcun River has cut deep clefts into a soft substrate. In these horizontal swaths of space, the village of Setenil is tucked – or perhaps grew is a better description. Inhabited since prehistory, it was natural for man to take refuge under the immense granite cornice. Unlike other troglydite villages, no further excavation was necessary. The overhanging rock became a roof, the linear caves became the rooms, the riverbed, a floor, a roadway, the front yard. Nature and architecture meld here, each becoming the other, together becoming something new.

Above and around these semi-subterranean structures more conventional buildings have been built as the town has grown, and they peacefully co-exist, neither commanding more prestige, each respecting the other, each a part of the whole that is this beautiful town. The first glimpse of Setenil, the long, horizontal line of white inside the land, is breathtaking; it takes a moment to realize exactly what has happened here. It looks like, feels like, life, emerging from the earth; it is like cutting a kiwi open – the amazing surprise of that brilliantly colorful fruit within that rough, brown skin. The simple relationship, that which contains, that which is contained, the inherently contrasting qualities, yet this land and this village share a completely appropriate embrace.

298

The river flows calmly

in its own season,

dry in summer,

with a series of simple

arched bridges

that keep both sides

of this village

bound together,

tying more than

the halves of a village...

they bind the inhabitants

to the land, the families to each other...

they link history to today.

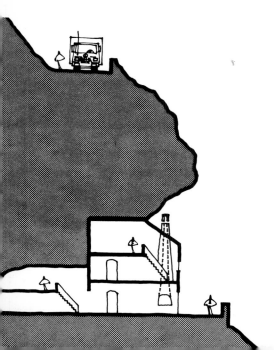

"Architecture is not art, it is a natural function.
It grows out of the ground like animals and plants, or
like a tree, that unfolds and develops, as long as the
man who planted it tends it with proper care."

Leger

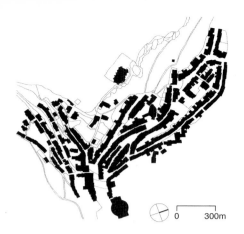

0   300m

Montefrio

Montefrio has been home to invaders from all sides in the long history of Spain, yet is remote enough from the rest of the world to retain its picturesque charm. A massive, wedge shaped rock outcropping is crowned with the majestic, gothic fortress-church, La Villa. Like necklaces of glistening jewels, rows of whitewashed houses quietly drape the lower slopes, connecting the dramatic mountain to the rolling brown countryside in terraced layers. The tawny color of the land flows into and over the village in waves of tile roofs. There is a powerful dialogue between color and texture, horizontal and vertical, ordinary and extraordinary, traditional and contemporary, simplicity and complexity, tactile and spiritual, dream and reality, past and future, a dialogue that inspires calm, contemplation. Simple joys enrich the days, the early morning sounds of women sweeping the doorsteps, the sweet taste of figs and fresh lemonade in the shade of a fragrant citrus tree, arranging flowers clipped moments ago from the garden below our window.

An iridescent shimmer in the heat rising from the town is like a gossamer veil that sharpens and softens reality in Montefrio. Patterns lie like delicate ornamentation on unadorned surfaces. Textures abound in the shadows of the roof tiles, the framework of a wagon, a sweep of trees against the hillside, the farmhouse in the field, the orchards beyond, in the bricks and rubble of an old wall...unpretentious elements that speak simply but with knowing – they change with the sun, with the season – they disappear – only to reappear with a surprise in another composition on another day.

304

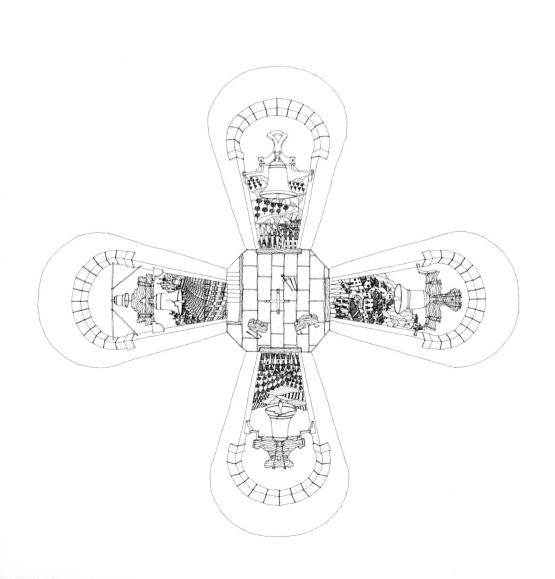

Simple streets with

little articulation

to give them

visual distinction

are vital,

thriving elements

of village life;

the evening promenade

and clusters of people

at each doorstep

make the street

a prime social

gathering place,

flowing between

the buildings

like a lifeblood,

making these villages

more than living places –

they become living beings.

"The master artisan participates in the creative process through traditional rituals which prepare him to create works of art that reflect in the world of the imagination. These rituals relate man to the rhythms of nature and the cosmos, whose solitude and serenity provide the first step in his spiritual ascent. The traditional man seeks to build a world through art that reflects equilibrium, serenity and peace."

Nader Ardalan & Laheh Bakhtiar

by Cathi House

Reflections

One of those moments that changed our life was a well choreographed event, planned by the fates, for we could not have even imagined what wonders awaited us. We went to Europe as young architects just out of school. Months of travel through central Europe, seeing all the grand cities and classical architecture, took us into the winter. Cold and tired, we headed south, to Greece, thinking we would see the Parthenon then relax on a beautiful warm beach for a week. Our first vision of Greece was in the morning light from a ferry gliding through the Ionian Islands and the villages on the northwestern coast. Arriving in Athens at midnight, we awakened to the Acropolis sparkling just outside our window. A photograph of overwhelming beauty in our hotel room led us to the island of Santorini, in the group of Aegean Islands known as the Cyclades. The first morning on Santorini was one of those moments that changed our lives forever. Stepping out onto our balcony, we saw a stairway, an organic sculpture, carved into the cliff. The power and beauty of that stairway took our breath away, and that moment's intense poetic impact propelled our lives onto a path we could not have imagined. To think of Greece is to ponder classical architecture, sculpture, literature, poetry, and the birth of ideals that transformed the world. To experience Greece is to see with a rare clarity. It is impossible to truly convey the beauty, power, and significance of this magical place. Greece was our first love as architects and as inhabitants of this world.

When we decided to rent a house on Santorini, I made a list of minimum necessary conveniences – hot and cold running water, heat, a refrigerator, a stove...The second house we saw was inhabited by mules with sprouting onions scattered around. It had no plumbing, no appliances, no heat, minimal electricity, and a straw mattress on an old iron bed...We fell in love with it instantly and anything it lacked couldn't change the fact that this house was perfect for us. In our 800-year-old house, part cave, part built, clinging to the cliff 1,000 feet above the blue Aegean with a terrace facing the sunset, we discovered the depth to which thoughtfully conceived architecture can move one's soul. That home became our instructor. It continues to teach us. We went for a week and stayed for six months. We went as naive young architects and left with a vision of what architecture can and should be.

We have had the pleasure of several long, lingering trips through Italy, a living museum of art, history, and architecture. Exploring the refined details of Siena, the rugged simplicity of Pesche, the unique constructions around Alberobello, revealed the extraordinary richness of this prodigious land. In Assisi we rented a tiny stone cube hanging on an ancient wall overlooking the town, former servants' quarters to a grand mansion. We spent our days photographing, sketching, and exploring every winding passage. In remote villages of the Gran Sasso mountains we often stayed in private homes, an intimate way to experience the richness that unfolds when you get past the surface of what things 'look' like to what they 'are.' At the heel of Italy the Apulian countryside is dotted with the black conical roofs of trulli farmhouses in breathtaking compositions. Climbing through vineyards one day, photographing, life took a pleasant turn when we were spotted by a joyful group celebrating the harvest. They invited us to join them and we dined on plate after delicious plate prepared over an open fire on the terrace, while inside the rustic stone exterior of their ancient home, their well-equipped, sleek, contemporary kitchen looked like something out of the latest Italian design journal.

Our entry into what was then called Yugoslavia began on a cold winter day after weeks of travel in central Europe. We headed south to cross the Alps in a blizzard, through snowdrifts several feet deep. As evening approached, a glow appeared in the gray sky, a line of silvery light, a slit in heaven that tore open and released its treasure of crystalline blue sky and shafts of brilliant sunlight, and, as we descended the last slope, a row of cypress trees, the glistening Adriatic, and the Istrian Peninsula welcomed us into Yugoslavia. This is a land rich in history, beautiful villages, and gracious inhabitants. During weeks spent weaving our way down the Dalmatian Coast, exploring islands and coastal villages, curious onlookers would gather to watch us sketch and offer suggestions of other places to see. It was a glorious journey through a beautiful land. The conflict that later devastated this region filled us with great sorrow, sadness for the hatred of war, for the personal losses suffered, and for the destruction of so many sacred places and irreplaceable works of architecture.

Marks left by invaders from the Romans to the Moors are reminders that Spain has hosted many civilizations. Where, in Greek villages the whitewashed buildings sparkle in sharp contrast to their landscape, and in Italian hill towns the rough stone walls blend peacefully

with theirs, the villages of Andalusian Spain do both. Waves of roof tiles the color of the brown earth are slashed with swaths of brilliant white walls, melding the two into compositions that are both powerful and serene. Andalucia is a land of rugged harshness dotted with beautiful villages built in magnificent settings for protection and contained existence in a time of invasion and political struggle. They sparkle still, protecting the gentle worlds within from a new brand of invaders, tourists.

The clarity, function, and beauty of these Mediterranean villages are lessons in more than architecture. They are living models of what life and community can be. They celebrate building traditions that are both practical and ingenious, responding not only to local climate, materials, and topography, but also intimately to the needs of the inhabitants with poetic insight — environments that are stimulating and immensely livable. We are contemporary California architects and our travels to remote villages continue to be our prime source of inspiration and personal growth, renewing our work, our visions, ourselves, allowing us to let go of preconceptions, see the world with clear eyes, and search beyond the limits our own imagination. Our souls as architects were born on Santorini. From that first step into the world of indigenous architecture, many more journeys have followed, exploring villages throughout the Mediterranean, and beyond, in our continuing search for understanding.

Acknowledgments

This book celebrates the poetry of stone and spirit that lives throughout the Mediterranean. As beautiful as the villages are, they are simply the stones. The spirit of these enchanted lands lives in the kind and generous inhabitants. Each day our odyssey was touched by countless people who shared so much with us – simple, yet unforgettable moments – fresh figs with a glass of wine, cookies and ice cold water, the key to a hidden treasure, a long walk to a place we never could have found, a gentle touch, a loving embrace, an invitation into their homes and their families. They welcomed us into their world and in it, we found ourselves. We offer a special thank you to Yannis Vlavianos, who, like Kazantzakis' "Zorba", took us, as young, naive architects, under his wings and showed us the true meaning of the Greek spirit. We are forever grateful to all of the people who shared their world with us and hope their presence is felt in these pages.

We are thankful to Bernard Rudofsky for his vision in bringing indigenous architecture to the forefront of architectural thought. His words taught us to see beyond the facade, into the magic and meaning behind the surface. We had the pleasure of meeting him in our home and sharing thoughts and experiences as he looked through our piles of drawings and photographs. His periodic letters always brought pause and deep reflection. We also want to thank Aris Konstantinidis, Norman Carver, and Myron Goldfinger; their insightful writings and photographs continue to inspire us.

We are indebted to our professors, Olivio and Lucy Ferrari, Tom Regan, Gene Egger, Harold Hill, Ellen Braaten, and Charles Burchard for opening our eyes to the questions, for, without the questions, we could never find the answers. We are grateful for our friends and colleagues who have encouraged us over the years in our journeys, several of whom were kind enough to review this manuscript and offer their advice – Diana and Marc Goldstein, Barry Brukoff, Tony Cohen, Masako Takahashi, Jeffrey Becom, Paul Laseau, Richard Whitaker, Kelly Condon, Amena Hajjar, Douglas Ward, Carol Morra, Robert Brorsen, and Chuck Bowden. We would like to offer special thanks to Merritt and Nancy Mann, who inspired us to follow our dreams and feel strong in our own path through life.

We would like to acknowledge the San Francisco Chapter of the American Institute of Architects for hosting the inaugural exhibition of *Mediterranean Indigenous Architecture: timeless solutions for the human habitat* and BPS of San Francisco for assistance in reproduction. We would also like to thank the numerous architects and agencies who assisted us with the maps and plans and the Croatian National Tourist Board for the aerial photograph of Trogir.

We are grateful to James Warfield, a kindred spirit, for his encouragement, for his passion for travel and discovery, and for his thoughtful introduction. We are thankful for Lucy Ferrari as a precious mentor and continuing guide in the art of seeing, and for her foreword to this book. We would like to offer our very special thanks to Paul Latham and Alessina Brooks and their staff at the Images Publishing Group and to Rod Gilbert of the Graphic Image Studio for their enthusiasm for this project and desire to bring this book to fruition.